Infinite Compassion, Endless Wisdom
菩 薩 行 證

Infinite Compassion, Endless Wisdom

The Practice of the Bodhisattva Path

By Venerable Master Hsing Yun

Edited by Tom Manzo and Shujan Cheng

Published by Buddha's Light Publishing, Los Angeles

© 2009 Buddha's Light Publishing
First edition 2009

By Venerable Master Hsing Yun
Cover designed by Rachel Xu
Book designed by Wan Kah Ong and John Gill

Published by Buddha's Light Publishing
3456 S. Glenmark Drive,
Hacienda Heights, CA 91745, U.S.A.
Tel: (626) 923-5144
Fax: (626) 923-5145
E-mail: itc@blia.org
Website: www.blpusa.com

Printed in Taiwan.

Library of Congress Cataloging-in-Publication Data
Xingyun, da shi.
[Pu sa xing zheng. English]
Infinite compassion, endless wisdom : the practice of the Bodhisattva path / by Venerable Master Hsing Yun ; edited by Tom Manzo and Shujan Cheng.
p. cm.
ISBN 978-1-932293-36-4
1. Bodhisattva stages (Mahayana Buddhism) 2. Spiritual life--Buddhism. I. Manzo, Tom. II. Cheng, Shujan. III. Title. IV. Title: Practice of the Bodhisattva path.

BQ4330.X5613 2009
294.3'444--dc22

2009009879

Acknowledgements

We received a lot of help from many people and we want to thank them for their efforts in making the publication of this book possible. We especially appreciate Venerable Tzu Jung, the Chief Executive of the Fo Guang Shan International Translation Center (F.G.S.I.T.C.), Venerable Hui Chi, Abbot of Hsi Lai Temple, and Venerable Yi Chao, Director of F.G.S.I.T.C. for their support and leadership; Tom Manzo and Shujan Cheng for their editing; Louvenia Ortega, John Gill, Michael Tran, Wan Kah Ong for proofreading and preparing the manuscript for publication; and Rachel Xu for her cover design. Our appreciation also goes to everyone who has supported this project from its conception to its completion.

Contents

Introduction

Infinite Compassion, Endless Wisdom: The Practice of the Bodhisattva Path presents a detailed introduction to the stages on the path to the Mahayana Buddhist ideal of liberating both the self and others as well as the history of the formation of different schools of Buddhism, and accounts of the lives of the Buddha, bodhisattvas and lay devotees.

The book begins by describing how the path should be approached, comparing the causes and conditions necessary for initiating spiritual development to the causes and conditions necessary for the intellectual formation required for professional success. Once the proper orientation to the path has been established, the text states in "The Practice of the Bodhisattva Path" that there are infinite ways of practice on the bodhisattva path; all of these, however, are embodied in the Four Universal Vows, the Four Immeasurable States of Mind, the Four Means of Embracing and the Six Perfections, and the text describes these in detail. The third section, "The Stages of the Bodhisattva Path" is based on the stages of spiritual development that the Buddha himself experienced prior to enlightenment, as narrated in the *Jataka* Tales, and describes the more than fifty levels before reaching the complete attainment of Buddhahood.

With this background established, the text then provides examples of five important bodhisattvas: Avalokitesvara

Bodhisattva, Manjusri Bodhisattva, Samantabhadra Bodhisattva, Ksitigarbha Bodhisattva, and Maitreya Bodhisattva. Any reader unfamiliar with these bodhisattvas will find a wealth of information about their significance in Buddhist traditions.

The text also provides biographies of spiritual leaders in the Mahayana Buddhist tradition. These include: Asvaghosa, who was also a Sanskrit poet, dramatist and musician; Nagarjuna, a prolific scholar known as "The Patriarch of Eight Schools," and also as the Patriarch of Esoteric Buddhism in Tibet; Aryadeva, who, following in the footsteps of Nagarjuna, advanced the Mahayana teaching of emptiness, and voluntarily served in the military in order to persuade a king, and by extension his subjects, to convert to Buddhism; Asanga and Vasubandhu, the two brothers who founded the "Consciousness Only" School; Queen Srimala, wife of a king and an early proponent of Sunday Schools and of prenatal care; and Vimalakirti, whose eponymous sutra demonstrates that a lay devotee can be as enlightened as a monastic.

The book also emphasizes the spiritual development of the young in "Young Bodhisattvas:" Sudhana, who traveled throughout India, meeting and studying with over fifty spiritual leaders, is an example of Buddhist spiritual study abroad; Yasa, who encountered the Buddha shortly after his Enlightenment and became a follower of the Buddha; Rahula, the Buddha's only son, who was ordained under the Buddha and became the youngest monastic; Sumaghadi, a young lady of profound wisdom, who attended the Buddha's Dharma assemblies and was not afraid to speak directly to the Buddha; Bhadda Kapilani, who, though young and beautiful and at one time betrothed to Mahakasyapa, joined him in being ordained by the Buddha; and the Celestial Maiden, who rained flowers on Sariputra, much to his (initial) dismay. The tales bring Buddhism to life, and help the reader see some of the rich traditions and personal accounts that are part of Mahayana Buddhism.

The text concludes with three important chapters: "The Characteristics of a Modern Bodhisattva," which states that modern bodhisattvas must have a cheerful personality, safeguard Buddhist teachings, practice their faith along Mahayana principles, and apply skill in means to liberate sentient beings; "Attributes of a Bodhisattva," which describes how bodhisattvas have the endowment of great roots, possession of great wisdom, faith and conviction in the Great Dharma, perception of the Great Truth, cultivation of magnanimous acts, endurance of an extremely long period of cultivation, and attainment of Buddhahood; and "The Completion of the Bodhisattva Path," which describes attainment of the bodhisattva path in the family, society, and the Dharma Realms.

Anyone interested in learning about Buddhism will find the combination of basic theoretical framework, practical application, and historical knowledge a useful introduction and overview. Readers who are already Buddhist and are sincere in dedicating themselves to the cultivation of the bodhisattva path will find this book compelling. The book provides not just the fundamental principles, but also extensive references to the Buddhist canon, and both the basic principles as well as advanced methods that they can follow.

— Tom Manzo

CHAPTER ONE

The First Step on the
Bodhisattva Path

The term "*bodhisattva*" originated in India. "*Bodhi*" is translated as "awakened" or "enlightened," and "*sattva*" as "sentient being." Anyone who is awakened to worldly impermanence, emptiness and suffering, and who therefore resolves to attain Buddhahood and liberate sentient beings, can be called a bodhisattva. Whether one has been ordained is not important, nor is one's status; as long as one has initiated the resolve to attain bodhicitta, one is eligible to be called a bodhisattva.

Let us begin with the first step on the bodhisattva path — the causes and conditions conducive to the initiation of bodhicitta. No one is born a bodhisattva. There is a saying, "There is not a naturally born Maitreya or Sakyamuni." The breadth of a bodhisattva's cultivation through many *kalpas* and countless lifetimes, from the initial causes to the ultimate attainment of Buddhahood, can be broken down into fifty-one levels.[1] This is a long journey that involves the persistent and arduous practice of a wide range of deeds that are beneficial to sentient beings.

---

[1] See chapter 3

Before one can qualify to become a university professor, one would have to undergo primary education as a child and secondary education in the teens, gradually moving on to higher education and research at the university to obtain master's and doctorate degrees. However, the accomplishment of this long academic career is dependent not only on the ability of the individual, but also on the support afforded by the individual's parents, teachers, and society as a whole. In the same way, to attain the bodhisattva state that immediately precedes the equal enlightenment of Buddhahood, initiating bodhicitta is the necessary and crucial first step. It is of immense importance at this starting point not to deviate from the right path. The following are some guidelines to prevent us from straying off course:

1. Do not tread the bodhisattva path for the sake of fame or fortune; do not indulge in worldly desires. One should embark on the bodhisattva path solely to attain Buddhahood and liberate sentient beings. This is the right way to initiate bodhicitta.

2. Have no apprehension about the long path of cultivation and the difficulty of liberating sentient beings; only be concerned about the posterity of the Dharma and the well-being of living beings. This is the true initiation of bodhicitta.

3. Do not seek only for liberation of the self or for accomplishment within this life; only aim to exercise compassion and wisdom at will to attain the bodhi path. This is the great initiation of bodhicitta.

4. Do not linger in the merit of being reborn in the human and heavenly realms; do not aim to become only sravakas or pratyekabuddhas. Go forth on the bodhisattva path for the

perfect attainment of enlightenment and the possession of all virtues. This is the complete and perfect initiation of bodhicitta.

Those who have set their minds on the bodhi path need to sustain their resolve, treat the suffering of others as their own, and utilize their inner resources. With great compassion for the suffering of the world, and with the spirit to protect the Dharma, they should resolve to practice diligently to end their own afflictions and the cycle of birth and death, while also helping others to remove themselves from defilements so that they too can end their afflictions and attain happiness. In the *Treatise on the Exposition of the Perfection of Wisdom* (*Abhisamayalankara Sastra*), it is said that "the wisdom of bodhisattvas is not rooted in being, and their compassion does not abide in nirvana." It is only by exercising both compassion and wisdom without attaching to either existence or emptiness that the spirit of the bodhisattva can be freely and unreservedly mobilized for the benefit of all sentient beings.

The great master Shengan of the Qing Dynasty listed ten causes and conditions that give rise to bodhicitta. They are:

1. Being mindful of our gratitude towards the Buddha
2. Being mindful of our gratitude towards our parents
3. Being mindful of our gratitude towards our teachers
4. Being mindful of our gratitude towards the givers of alms
5. Being mindful of our gratitude towards sentient beings
6. Being mindful of the suffering of life and death
7. Having respect for our own spiritual being
8. Being repentant of our karmic hindrances
9. Aspiring towards rebirth in the Pure Land

10. Being mindful of the importance of preserving the wholesome Dharma for a long time

The initiation of bodhicitta should be founded on loving kindness, compassion and skillful means. Hence, it is the fostering of loving kindness and compassion, coupled with skillful means that sets up the first step of the bodhisattva path. Bodhicitta is not aroused out of an impulse of the moment, it is the result of consistently upholding the following in everyday life: not forsaking any sentient being; not dismissing the slightest of good deeds; taking guidance in the Buddha's teachings; cultivating with reference to the truth. Only when we practice the bodhisattva path in this way can we avoid falling into a boundless sea of suffering.

The past sages of great virtue who gave rise to bodhicitta and practiced on the path can serve as the best examples for our own cultivation. It is recorded in the *Jataka Stories* (*Jatakas*) that, in fulfilling his great vow of "giving charity" as a bodhisattva, the Buddha, in his past lives, fed a tiger[2] and an eagle[3] with his own body and flesh. In another life, as Ksantyrsi, he accomplished his practice by breeding neither anger nor hatred when he was mutilated by Kaliraja. Sariputra went all the way up north on his own to supervise the construction of the Jetavana Vihara.[4] He also had to confront the fierce challenge of the six heterodox groups, and eventually subdued them with his great powers. Maudgalyayana was martyred because of his faith when heretical followers attacked him for his defense of the Buddha's teachings.[5] Purna took it upon himself to travel to the

---

[2] See the *Sutra of Golden Light*, chapter 4.
[3] See the *Treatise on the Stories of the Previous Births of Bodhisattvas*, chapter 1.
[4] See the *Sutra on the Wise and the Foolish*, chapter 10.
[5] See the *Gradual Discourses of the Buddha*, chapter 18.

barbaric regions of Sunaparantaka to spread the Dharma, at a great risk to his own safety.[6] Mahanaman submerged himself in deep waters to save his fellow clansmen, and others like Sudatta donated all his possessions as alms. All these acts were motivated by bodhicitta, without which such great deeds would never have been accomplished.

There were also many historical incidents in China that demonstrated the selflessness of individuals who practiced the bodhisattva path for the cause of perpetuating the Buddha's teachings. The starting point on the bodhisattva path is to be aware of one's own ignorance, defilements, limited abilities and imperfections, and to thus diligently and extensively learn the Dharma, to promote the earnest resolve to cultivate the Buddha way and to further extend this bodhisattva spirit to the liberation of all beings.

---

[6] See the *Connected Discourses of the Buddha*, chapter 13.

Chapter Two

The Practice of the
Bodhisattva Path

In Buddhist cultivation, the practice of sravakas and pratyekabuddhas for self-enlightenment is not the complete and perfect Dharma. Only through the vow to practice the Six Perfections (*Paramitas*) of the Mahayana bodhisattva path, can one liberate both oneself and others and fully attain Buddhahood.

We have examined the causes and conditions for initiating bodhicitta, and have prescribed guidelines not only for discerning the right motives for its initiation, but also for distinguishing the true motives from the false ones, those that are great from those that are small, and the partial from the complete. Let us now turn to the actual practice of the bodhisattva path. In the *Vimalakirti Sutra* (*Vimalakirtinirdesa Sutra*), it says that "the mind that is upright is the bodhisattva path; the mind that is profound is the bodhisattva path; the mind that aspires to bodhi is the bodhisattva path; the mind that conquers *mara* is the bodhisattva path."[7] Although there are

---

[7] The "upright mind" is the honest, straight, and truthful. The "profound mind" searches and firmly believes in the Way. The "mind that aspires to bodhi" strives to uphold and practice what is learned. The "mind that conquers *mara*" destroys *mara* by resisting temptation.

infinite ways to practice on the bodhisattva path, all of them are in fact embodied within the Four Universal Vows, the Four Immeasurable States of Mind, the Four Means of Embracing and the Six Perfections. These are the central practices for every bodhisattva that resolves to attain supreme and perfect enlightenment.

The Four Universal Vows

The Four Universal Vows are the Mahayana vows initiated through devout earnestness as a result of a deep understanding of the Four Noble Truths — the truth of suffering, the cause of suffering, the cessation of suffering, and the path leading to the cessation of suffering.

- Since the suffering of sentient beings is immense, a bodhisattva vows to help liberate limitless sentient beings from their suffering.
- Since suffering is accumulated through unwholesome karma, a bodhisattva vows to help sentient beings sever the endless flow of afflictions.
- In order to guide sentient beings toward the path of cultivation, a bodhisattva vows to learn the infinite Dharma.
- In order to help sentient beings realize the fruit of cultivation, a bodhisattva vows to attain supreme Buddhahood.

Mahayana bodhisattvas who have initiated bodhicitta as a result of practicing the Four Universal Vows should apply these vows to propagate the true meaning of the Four Noble Truths.

The Four Immeasurable States of Mind

These refer to the immeasurable states of loving kindness, compassion, joy, and equanimity. In practicing the Four Immeasurable States of Mind, the defilements of greed, anger, ignorance, and arrogance dissipate, and one realizes the boundless state of the bodhisattva.

- Immeasurable loving kindness is practiced to give confidence and faith to others.
- Immeasurable compassion is practiced to give hope to others.
- Immeasurable joy is practiced to give others happiness.
- Immeasurable equanimity is to use skillful means and to give convenience to others.

Bodhisattvas realize that life and death are like a flickering flame and understand the suffering that accompanies them. However, in order to uphold the vow to eliminate suffering and bring happiness, bodhisattvas look upon the elderly as their parents and the young as their children. They do not stop at liberating themselves, but are committed to liberating all sentient beings from suffering. In the *Collection of Dharanis* the magnanimous mind of a bodhisattva is compared to the expanse of the earth, the depth of the oceans, the usefulness of a bridge or ferry in crossing to the other shore, and the vastness of space itself. As such, bodhisattvas are forever nurturing wholesome Dharmas; they can embrace all differences; they can induce all happiness, and they can accomplish everything, regardless of the causes and conditions.

The Four Means of Embracing

The Four Means of Embracing are skillful means employed by bodhisattvas to liberate sentient beings of varying capacities and inclinations from ignorance to enlightenment. This is described in the *Lotus Sutra* (*Saddharmapundarika Sutra*) as "first tempt him with desire, then lead him to the Buddha's wisdom."

* Giving: this is an act of creating affinities with others. All lawful and ethical requests by others should be fulfilled to the best of one's efforts. These include material gifts, sharing the Dharma and giving fearlessness. With loving kindness and compassion, bodhisattvas will bring happiness to people who learn from them, hence inspiring others to cultivate bodhicitta.
* Kind words: When spoken as a skillful means, kind words can be very beneficial. Loving and caring words can evoke joy; words of compassion and praise can offer confidence; and citing the words of sages and saints can inspire intrepidness. These kinds of speech will bring people closer to the bodhisattvas, hence increasing their contact with and receptiveness to the Dharma.
* Altruism and beneficence: these include mental, physical and verbal acts of benevolence. Right mindfulness, right action and right speech bring benefit to sentient beings, who will hence be inspired to vow to initiate bodhicitta.
* Sympathy and empathy: an example of this is the bodhisattvas' power of making vows to manifest in innumerable forms within the six realms of existence so that sentient beings may see a glimpse of light in the darkness, get help in desperation find reliance in desolation and obtain liberation from suffering.

The Six Perfections

The Sanskrit word for perfection, *"paramita,"* is literally translated as "gone to the other shore" and conveys the meaning of liberation. The Six Perfections are for leading the deluded to enlightenment, the heretical onto the right path, the suffering to happiness, and all sentient beings from this shore of affliction to the other shore of liberation. The Six Perfections constitute the six forms of practice for bodhisattvas to attain Buddhahood.

- Giving: Giving is having a generous mind and giving without attachment to form. Any form of giving should be carried out without clinging to the thought of what has been given, who is giving, and to whom the gift is given. This should be the way by which bodhisattvas practice the perfection of giving.

- Upholding the precepts: The precepts are forms of moral discipline that are upheld out of respect for all beings. This involves observance of the Buddhist precepts, acting in accordance with wholesome Dharma, and practice in benefiting sentient beings. Such is the conduct of bodhisattvas in the practice of this perfection.

- Patience: Patience is enduring hardship with equanimity. It is a practice whereby there is tolerance in situations of persecution, acceptance in circumstances of adversity, and sustained contemplation on the truth of all phenomena. The practice of this perfection calls for determined patience and perseverance.

- Diligence: Diligence is having a fearless mind that eliminates wrongdoing and practices good deeds. In cultivating their path, bodhisattvas must diligently practice courage and bravery, diligently practice wholesome Dharmas, and diligently practice bringing joy and benefit to others. They do not grow weary of teaching the obstinate but will apply their efforts ceaselessly.

- Meditation: Meditation is applying right mindfulness without duality. Bodhisattvas achieve stable and secure concentration for themselves and others and practice the three progressive levels of meditation that pertain to the mundane, the supramundane and the supernatural states of being.

- Prajna wisdom: Prajna wisdom is great wisdom that encompasses the understanding of both emptiness and existence without either one hindering the other. Bodhisattvas propagate the Dharma through their use of the prajna of language, the prajna of contemplation, and the prajna of true reality,[8] and skillfully apply their wisdom to incite in sentient beings benevolent mindfulness so that they never lapse into suffering.

Thus, as one sutra says, "The initial resolve to cultivate is like the morning dew." Practitioners must strengthen their resolve to prevent retrogression on the bodhisattva path. The Four Universal Vows should be taken as the virtuous goal of their conduct; the Four Immeasurable States of Mind should be treated as the wondrous ways to bring happiness to all; the Four Means of Embracing should be cherished as the most precious blessings and wisdom; and the Six Perfections should be viewed as the kindly vessel that can liberate all beings from suffering. In addition to these, bodhisattvas should also take guidance from

---

[8] *The Explanation of the Diamond Wisdom Sutra* by Venerable Master Zhiyi of the Sui Dynasty.

the *Diamond Sutra*'s (*Vajracchedika Prajnaparamita Sutra*) exposition on prajna wisdom, which says, "no notion of self, a person, sentient beings or longevity." Moreover, bodhisattvas should be in accord with the view of great compassion as stipulated in the *Surangama Sutra*, which says, "As long as there is one other sentient being left unaccomplished in Buddhahood, [I] will not enter *nirvana*."

In the daily life of bodhisattvas, conditioned dharmas are seen as dreams, illusions, bubbles, and shadows. Their minds are not tainted by the five desires, and they always abide in right mindfulness. However, they take advantage of this worldly existence as their platform to teach and propagate the Dharma. There is a saying, "Even if there is a burning hot iron wheel above the head, it will not render suffering or caue one to retreat from bodhicitta." This well illustrates the maxim by which bodhisattvas pursue their noble mission to "liberate oneself and liberate others, awaken oneself and awaken others."

Chapter Three

The Stages on the
Bodhisattva Path

The Mahayana conception of the bodhisattva stems from the Buddha's own account of his past deeds, which served as the causes that led to his attainment of Buddhahood. In the *Jataka Stories*, one of the twelve sections of the Buddhist Canon, there are many references to beings who resolve to accomplish the Buddha way and cultivate diligently and relentlessly, often risking their own lives for the benefit of sentient beings. This is the spirit of the Mahayana Bodhisattva. From a bodhisattvas' first initiation of bodhicitta, he will have to practice the Four Universal Vows, the Four Immeasurable States of Mind, the Four Means of Embracing, and the Six Perfections in his own stride. Such a bodhisattva is like a new pupil climbing up the grades at school, having to go through fifty-one levels of cultivation before reaching the complete attainment of Buddhahood.

According to the *Medallion Sutra on the Bodhisattva Path*, there are fifty-two levels of cultivation on the bodhisattva path. There are ten levels of faith, ten levels of dwelling, ten levels of practice, ten levels of dedication, ten levels of ground, the level of equal enlightenment, and the level of supreme enlightenment. During this long process of cultivation, it is essential to remain consistently diligent, self-critical, motivated, and self-validated. The following is a summary of the progressive levels of cultivation on the bodhisattva path.

Ten levels of Faith

The *Flower Ornament Sutra* (*Avatamsaka Sutra*) says, "Faith is the source of the Way, and the mother of virtues. It fosters and nurtures all wholesome Dharmas, dispels doubt and allows detachment from desires, hence opening up the ultimate path to nirvana." As faith is the first step on the path, the fifty-two levels in the development of the bodhisattva begin with the ten levels of faith. The most important objective of cultivating the ten levels of faith is to prevent retrogression. The ten levels of faith are:

1.   faith
2.   mindfulness
3.   diligence
4.   upholding precepts
5.   meditative concentration
6.   wisdom
7.   protection of the truth
8.   resolute vow
9.   non-retrogression
10. dedication of merits

To enter the gates of the bodhisattva path with confidence, practitioners need to take refuge in the Triple Gem. Thereafter, they must be constantly mindful of the Dharma, energetically practice the Four Immeasurable States of Mind, strictly uphold the precepts, meditate to gain concentration, study the sutras of prajna wisdom, protect and defend right views, and vow with great resolve to accomplish the Buddha way without retrogression. Finally, they must dedicate the virtues accrued from their practice to the beings of all dharma realms in the hope of liberating them from their afflictions. Only after practicing the above for one *asamkheya* (great) kalpa, can a bodhisattva truly achieve unfailing faith in the precepts and the Buddha, Dharma, and Sangha.

Ten levels of dwelling

For a bodhisattva to attain virtues, faith must securely abide in his or her mind. To secure a stable and peaceful mind, bodhisattvas must uphold precepts with purity and without transgression, be patient and gentle, practice equality and generosity with prajna wisdom, and aspire to advance in the ten levels of dwelling. The ten levels of dwelling are:

1. *The vow of initiation*: In this dwelling, one must believe in the Triple Gem and all wholesome dharmas and not learn any unwholesome dharmas. In this way, the mind will give rise to all virtues. Beginning with a vow of initiation, the bodhisattva needs to:

   i.   abide in a magnanimous mind
   ii.   abide in a pure mind
   iii.   abide in unobstructed cultivation
   iv.   abide in a noble place
   v.   abide in skillful means
   vi.   abide in right-mindedness
   vii.   abide in non-retrogression
   viii. abide in the bodhisattva path
   ix.   abide in commitment to accomplishment
   x.   abide in the state of coronation

Abiding in the above, bodhisattvas with bodhicitta would unmistakably enter the path to Buddhahood with unfailing faith in the precepts and the Buddha, Dharma, and Sangha. They will settle securely in meditative concentration and Dharma joy, as well as be constantly mindful of the Three Dharma Seals, Four Noble Truths, and the vows of compassion. They will possess innumerable skillful means and have profound understanding of prajna wisdom, emptiness, and equality. They will engage in giving without attachment to form, and have pure conduct of body, mind and speech. In other words, they will be on the right course for the Mahayana path.

2. *Preparing the foundation*: In this dwelling, bodhisattvas apply the mind of emptiness to purify all dharmas. The bodhisattva's mind becomes as bright and pure as a pure crystal, capable of manifesting within it fine gold.

3. *Cultivation of virtue*: Having completed the first two levels of dwelling, the bodhisattva practices with wisdom and travels freely in all directions.

4. *Noble birth*: Due to the bodhisattva's previous wondrous practices they live in accordance with the Dharma and will be born as a Buddhist and become the prince of the Dharma.

5. *Skillful means*: Because they have practiced infinite wholesomeness, the bodhisattva can benefit himself and others, be complete in skillful means, and have a dignified appearance.

6. *Right mind*: Having already achieved prajna wisdom, the bodhisattva not only has a dignified appearance, but his mind is the same as the Buddha's.

7. *Non-retrogression*: Having already reached the realm that is without birth and is ultimately empty, their mind constantly fulfills the vow of emptiness and formlessness. Body and mind are one, and they grow in the Dharma everyday.

8. *Youthful nature*: From the initial vow to non-retrogression, the evil mind no longer arises and the bodhi mind is never violated. At this level of dwelling, the bodhisattva has completed the Buddha's bodhi and vows, and has a body that has the Buddha's manifestations, presence, dignity, power, and the ability to appear as sentient beings wish. The bodhisattva has also attained the Buddha's virtues, wisdom, and Dharma body.

9. *Prince of the Dharma*: Having entered and been nurtured in the noble womb through the previous levels of dwelling, the bodhisattva is now born. Having understood the doctrine from the Buddha, the bodhisattva now prepares to succeed him.

10. *Coronation*: In this level of dwelling, the bodhisattva becomes the son of the Buddha and can now engage in his affairs. The Buddha thus anoints the bodhisattva with the water of wisdom.

Ten levels of practice

After having accomplished the ten levels of faith and the ten levels of dwelling, bodhisattvas further need to learn the more specific methods of cultivation toward the path of Buddhahood through the ten levels of practice. The ten levels of practice are:

1. *Joyfulness*: In this level of practice, the bodhisattva practices to bring joy to all sentient beings.

2. *Benefiting others*: In this level of practice, the bodhisattva practices to bring benefit to all sentient beings.

3. *No contradictions*: In this level of practice, the bodhisattva practices the Dharma without contradictions.

4. *Resilience*: In this level of practice, the bodhisattva will no longer succumb to difficulties he encounters or surrender his initial resolve.

5. *Non-ignorance and non-confusion*: In this level of practice, the bodhisattva is no longer deluded by ignorance or confusion.

6. *Appearing in any form at will*: In this level of practice, the bodhisattva manifests every possible good in their conduct.

7. *Non-attachment*: In this level of practice, the bodhisattva cultivates purity and non-attachment.

8. *Exalting what is most difficult*: In this level of practice, the bodhisattva is able to attain what is most difficult.

9.   *Perfecting wholesome Dharmas:* In this level of practice, the bodhisattva perfects all wholesome Dharmas.

10. *Truly practicing the path:* In this level of practice, the bodhisattva achieves the supramundane truth, and practice and teaches the supramundane truth.

Ten levels of dedicating merits

Having completed cultivation on the ten levels of faith, the ten levels of dwelling, and the ten levels of practice, it is essential that bodhisattvas reinforce the merits and wisdom attained by fulfilling the ten levels of dedicating merits. This means dedicating one's virtues accrued from wholesome practice toward all sentient beings, which in turn will enable the bodhisattvas to enter into nirvana. The following are the ten levels of dedicating merits:

1.   *Rescuing and protecting:* In this level of dedicating merit, the bodhisattva vows with great compassion to rescue and protect all sentient beings.

2.   *Unfailing faith:* In this level of dedicating merit, the bodhisattva will never destroy any merit or virtue derived from any wholesome Dharma.

3.   *Being at peace and in harmony:* In this level of dedicating merit, the bodhisattva transfers his merits to others with peace and harmony.

4.   *Reaching all:* In this level of dedication of merit, the bodhisattva makes all his good deeds truly reach all sentient beings.

5. *Infinite wholesomeness*: In this level of dedication of merit, the bodhisattva gives everything to all sentient beings without reservation.

6. *Affirming wholesomeness*: In this level of dedication of merit, the bodhisattva affirms his vow to practice for himself and others.

7. *Adaptability*: In this level of dedication of merit, the bodhisattva initiates the mind to follow wholesome karma, wherever it may be, without rejecting anyone's wishes.

8. *Achieving suchness*: In this level of dedication of merit, the bodhisattva transfers his merit so that all beings may attain Buddhahood.

9. *Liberation*: In this level of dedicating of merit, the bodhisattva transfers his merit so that everyone can be liberated.

10. *Achieving equanimity*: In this level of dedication of merit, the bodhisattva transfers his merit with the wish that the dharma realm becomes equal and complete.

Bodhisattvas entering this stage would vow with great compassion to rescue and protect all sentient beings. They will never destroy any merits or virtues derived from all wholesome Dharmas, but will transfer them to others with peace and harmony. They will attempt to ensure that all good deeds are done and that the merits so accrued will reach all. They will make the unwavering vow to do good deeds as well as to help others to do the same. They will aspire to the mind of acting in accord with wholesome Dharmas and not in opposition to sentient beings' goals. In addition, they need to dedicate the merits to all sentient beings toward Buddhahood and attaining liberation. Their intention is to enable all dharma realms to be in equanimity and completion. Bodhisattvas are able to be detached from the forms of sentient beings, and enter their Dharma nature. Within their Dharma nature, they no longer discriminate between friends or foes, treating all sentient beings as family, and never destroying or detracting from their bodhisattva vows. Finally, they dedicate their merits to rescuing and protecting all sentient beings. Therefore, the bodhisattva will inspire the mind to fulfill the Mahayana path; maintaining a mind of equanimity without delusion or confusion; a mind without any bonds or attachments to the cycle of birth and death, to friends and foes, to love and hatred, or to wholesomeness and unwholesomeness. Their great and boundless vows will reach all dharma realms equally, and treat self and others as one.

Ten levels of ground

Upon completion of the cultivation of the stages of faith, dwelling, practice, and dedicating merits, bodhisattvas enter the ten levels of ground whereby profound wisdom is attained and all defilements eliminated. They are in a state of constant mindfulness of loving kindness and compassion, totally absorbed in gentleness. Dwelling amidst people of all types and relationships, they are completely and freely at ease with them. The ten levels of ground are:

1. *Joy:* The first ground is when bodhisattvas experience great joyfulness as a result of their of their entrance into the initial stage of realization.

2. *Freedom from defilement*: The second ground is when bodhisattvas depart from defilement, unwholesomeness, and immorality, enabling them to completely uphold the precepts of purity and be free from all defilement.

3. *Radiance*: The third ground is when bodhisattvas have already gone through the methods of listening, contemplation, and practice, and finally realize the truth and attain the radiance of the Dharma.

4. *Brilliant wisdom*: The fourth ground is when bodhisattvas first ignite the flame of wisdom and eliminate all their mental afflictions. With their afflictions eliminated, the light of wisdom will shine even brighter.

5. *Mastery of final difficulties*: The fifth ground is when bodhisattvas attain supramundane wisdom, enabling them to liberate obstinate sentient beings.

6. *Manifestation of prajna wisdom*: The sixth ground is when bodhisattvas enter the profound Dharma through listening to the perfection of prajna wisdom, after which the great prajna wisdom is manifested.

7. *Proceeding afar*: The seventh ground is when bodhisattvas have already attained the profound wisdom of skillful means and gain brightness from the patient resting in the belief of no birth. They complete the merits and virtues of bodhi and fulfill the various great vows. They thus become more diligent in enhancing their cultivation.

8. *Attainment of calm*: The eighth ground is when the power of the bodhisattvas' fundamental vows result in the appearance of Buddhas before them, to teach them the wisdom of the Tathagatas. With this new wisdom bodhisattvas are able to manifest themselves in the ten directions within a single thought to teach and liberate countless sentient beings.

9. *Finest discriminatory wisdom*: The ninth ground is when bodhisattvas abide in wonderful wisdom and are known as the kings of the Dharma. They utilize the Dharmas of the Three Vehicles unrelentingly to liberate sentient beings as well as advising and guiding them according to their conditions and tendencies just as a cloud reaches out far and wide to cover every corner.

10. *Attainment of the fertilizing power of the Dharma-cloud*: The tenth ground is when bodhisattvas rely on non-outflow wisdom to eliminate all karmic delusions and hindrances and practice consistent with suchness. Covered by the great Dharma rain and the cloud of Buddhas, they gain the ten powers of the Tathagatas and complete the virtues of the noble fruits. The Bodhisattvas then use their *Dharmakaya* as clouds that will spread to all sentient beings and guide them to abide on the path of wisdom.

From initiation of bodhicitta to the cultivation of the fifty stages of faith, dwelling, practice, dedicating merits, and ground, bodhisattvas now reach the fifty-first level of equal enlightenment. This is the level attained after having accomplished the ten levels of ground, where their understanding and discernment of the Dharma is the same as that of the Buddhas. In this penultimate level, the Buddhas perceive them as bodhisattvas, while the less-cultivated bodhisattvas regard them as Buddhas. Finally, the bodhisattvas will move onto the fifty-second level of supreme enlightenment, after all the last traces of afflictions and ignorance have been eliminated, the wondrous prajna wisdom has been attained, and the truth of nirvana has been realized. This is also the same stage as the perfect enlightenment of the Buddha.

CHAPTER FOUR

Avalokitesvara

The Bodhisattva of Compassion

The image of the Avalokitesvara Bodhisattva is the most commonly seen in China. In crowded cities, small towns and aboard fishing boats, images of Avalokitesvara Bodhisattva can be found enshrined everywhere. The people of this Saha world are known to have a special affinity with this Bodhisattva.

In Chinese, Avalokitesvara Bodhisattva is known as Guanshiyin Pusa, which means "the Bodhisattva who observes and contemplates the sounds of the world." This implies that the Bodhisattva will come to the rescue of anyone who calls on Guanshiyin Pusa for help. The Bodhisattva is also known as Guanzizai, meaning "the Bodhisattva who observes freely at ease," because the Bodhisattva contemplates the truth, human beings, and phenomena, with a mind that is free from all defilements. Avalokitesvara Bodhisattva has many names, such as "the One of Fearless Giving,"[9] "the Bodhisattva of Great Compassion," "the Great One of Perfect Transcendence," and "the Guanyin of the South China Sea." As recorded in the *Sutra on the Great Compassion Dharani*, Avalokitesvara Bodhisattva

---

[9] "Fearless giving" means to dispel the fears of all beings and liberate them. The three kinds of giving are the giving of fearlessness, material goods, and the Dharma.

attained Buddhahood countless kalpas ago, and was then known as the Tathagata of Illuminating Right Dharma. But out of loving kindness and compassion for the sentient beings of this Saha world, he returned to liberate those that have an affinity with him.

A detailed description of the meritorious deeds of Avalokitesvara Bodhisattva is found in the *Chapter on the Universal Gate* of the *Lotus Sutra (Saddhamapundarika)*. It is almost a biographical account, with expositions on the Bodhisattva's many manifestations, great compassion, super-natural powers, and accounts of liberating sentient beings in various lands. It is recorded that Inexhaustible Intent Bodhi-sattva (*Aksayamati*) was so moved by the Buddha's exaltations on the deeds of Avalokitesvara Bodhisattva that an offering of ornaments was made to the latter as a token of respect and admiration. Dialogues in the sutra also project the image of Avalokitesvara Bodhisattva as a sacred one who exemplifies the skillful application of wisdom and compassion, as well as the skillful completion of wisdom and merit. For example, those who are mindful of the Bodhisattva will have their wish of having children fulfilled. As stated in the Chapter on the Universal Gate, "If any woman wishes for a son, she should pay homage and make offerings to Avalokitesvara Bodhisattva, and then she will bear a son endowed with merit, virtue, and wisdom. If any woman wishes for a daughter, she should make offerings to Avalokitesvara Bodhisattva, and then she will bear a beautiful and handsome daughter."

Avalokitesvara Bodhisattva can also help liberate sentient beings from the three poisons: "If any sentient beings have great sensual desires, they should contemplate Avalokitesvara Bodhisattva with reverence, and they will be free from desires. If they have great hatred and anger, they should contemplate Avalokitesvara Bodhisattva with reverence, and they will be free from anger. If they have great ignorance, they should contemplate Avalokitesvara Bodhisattva with reverence, and they will be free from ignorance." In addition, they will be relieved from the seven disasters brought about by fire, flood, hurricanes, warfare, demons, imprisonment, and criminals. In other words, sincerely contemplating the name of Avalokitesvara Bodhisattva will bring forth his great compassion, wisdom, and supernatural power to help remove them from these disasters. Thus the sutras state, "If sentient beings are in great distress, and immeasurable suffering afflicts them, the power of the wonderful wisdom of Avalokitesvara Bodhisattva will liberate them from the suffering of the world."

In addition to answering the earnest calls of sentient beings in crisis, Avalokitesvara Bodhisattva also teaches the Dharma to sentient beings based on their conditions and tendencies. The *Chapter on the Universal Gate* states that if anyone should need to be liberated by the form of a Buddha, Avalokitesvara Bodhisattva will manifest in the form of a Buddha to teach them the Dharma. If anyone should need to be liberated by the form of kings or emperors, he will manifest in the form of a king or an emperor to teach them the Dharma. Furthermore, if anyone should need to be liberated by the form of a *bhiksu* or *bhiksuni*, layman or laywoman, or a boy or girl, he will manifest in the necessary form to teach them the Dharma. In essence, Avalokitesvara Bodhisattva is able to manifest in thirty-three forms of transformation as a means of teaching sentient beings the Dharma and liberating them.

In regards to our faith toward Avalokitesvara Bodhisattva, the *Flower Ornament Sutra* states that, "[Avalokitesvara]

Bodhisattva is like the translucent moon that wanders ceaselessly across infinite space; when all defilements and impurities of the sentient mind have been cleansed, the bodhi-moon will brightly shine through." Therefore, when we hear the name of the Bodhisattva, we should recite his name and pay homage to him. At the same time, our mind will become pure, and with a concentrated mind, we can eliminate all delusion. We should also contemplate the great vows and deeds of Avalo-kitesvara Bodhisattva. Once we attain the above, the actions of our body, speech, and mind can become one. We should allow Avalokitesvara Bodhisattva's mind to be our mind, and let our mind be one with his.

Due to the widespread belief in Avalokitesvara Bodhisattva and the numerous sincere prayers of sentient beings, the Bodhisattva has manifested in various forms on countless occasions to help those that are suffering and in danger. Therefore there are numerous images of Avalokitesvara Bodhisattva's manifestations. For example, the Bodhisattva in white (*Baiyi Guanyin*), the Bodhisattva appearing in a bamboo grove (*Zhulin Guanyin*), the Bodhisattva holding a fishing basket (*Yulan Guanyin*), the Bodhisattva manifesting the water and the moon while sitting on a rock in the ocean (*Shuiyue Guanyin*), the Bodhisattva holding a crystal vase (*Liuli Guanyin*), the Bodhisattva manifesting from an open oyster shell (*Hali Guanyin*), the Bodhisattva bringing a child (*Songzi Guanyin*), the Bodhisattva manifesting as Mrs. Ma (*Malang Fu Guanyin*), the Bodhisattva with eleven faces (*Shiyi Mian Guanyin*), and the Bodhisattva of a thousand hands and eyes. Among these manifestations, most of them present the Bodhisattva with a noble female appearance. Hence, this was how the perception of the Bodhisattva as a woman began.

Actually, Avalokitesvara Bodhisattva's many manifestations are a skillful means of liberating sentient beings with varying needs and circumstances. Apart from appearing in the form of a king and a woman to teach the Dharma to sentient beings, the Bodhisattva has also manifested as a *deva*, a *vajra*-wielder, an *asura*, a dragon, a ghost, a snake, a bird, and many other forms. Therefore, the emphasis on whether Avalokitesvara Bodhisattva is a man or a woman is unimportant.

The assistance provided by Avalokitesvara Bodhisattva to the world exceeds all limitations. With fourteen kinds of fearlessness as well as a thousand hands and eyes, the Bodhisattva liberates sentient beings from suffering and danger with great compassion. In the *Record of the Manifestations of Avalokitesvara Bodhisattva* (*Guanyin Linggan Lu*), a number of stories depicting the Bodhisattva's manifestations are described. In one story, Emperor Wenzong of the Tang Dynasty stopped eating oysters after the Bodhisattva appeared to teach him. Another is about Chan Master Yongjue of the Song Dynasty who escaped injuries from torture during his imprisonment after frequently reciting the Bodhisattva's name for protection. Still another story tells of Dr. Sun Yat Sen's visit to Mount Putuo[10] where he saw the manifestation of the Bodhisattva. Yet another one describes a butcher who went on a pilgrimage and later became a filial son after being instructed by the Bodhisattva to regard and respect his own mother as a bodhisattva.

However, the true meaning of having faith in Avalokitesvara Bodhisattva is not to obtain aid but to conduct ourselves like him. In other words, like the Bodhisattva's ability to give fearlessness, we should also strengthen the power of our compassion, wisdom and courage to be a protector of sentient beings.

---

[10] Located in the Zhoushan Islands off the coast of Zhejiang Province.

*Like the Bodhisattva, we must give encouragement to the
distraught and dispirited.
Like the Bodhisattva, we must bring liberation and
sanctuary to those who are victimized.
Like the Bodhisattva, we must provide the unfortunate
with positive conditions and support.
Like the Bodhisattva, we must give guidance to those
who are lost and astray.*

CHAPTER FIVE

Manjusri

The Bodhisattva of Wisdom

In Sanskrit, the word Manjusri is interpreted as "wondrous virtues," "wondrous head," or "wondrous auspiciousness." The son of a respected family in Sravasti, Manjusri's birth was marked with many auspicious signs, and as a child he already possessed the thirty-two excellent marks of an enlightened one. Having accomplished the Way, Manjusri became the wisest disciple of the Buddha and was foremost among all bodhisattvas. Therefore, Manjusri is known as the "Prince of the Dharma." The Buddha once said that in one of his previous lives, he had received the Dharma from Manjusri. Therefore, Manjusri Bodhisattva is also known as "the Mother of Enlightenment of the three time periods," and in many sutras, the Bodhisattva is also recognized as the teacher of all Buddhas.

Manjusri Bodhisattva actually accomplished Buddhahood long ago. Both the Honored King of the Dragon Clan Tathagata mentioned in the *Surangama Samadhi Sutra* and the Buddha of Universal Illumination described in the *Repentance in the Names of the Eighty-Eight Buddhas* are actually represent-ations of Manjusri.

Manjusri Bodhisattva has many appearances, one of which has the Bodhisattva holding a lotus to denote nobleness and purity. Sometimes the Bodhisattva is seen as holding a sword to symbolize the severing of all afflictions with wisdom. Other images show Manjusri Bodhisattva on the back of a golden lion[11] to show his majestic courage, sitting on a lotus platform to symbolize purity without defilement, or riding on a peacock[12] to depict a free and easy flight.

Mount Wutai[13] in China is famously known as the place where Manjusri Bodhisattva has manifested in various forms to teach the Dharma. The image of Manjusri Bodhisattva as a monk can be found in the Sangha Hall and on the Ordination Altar within many Buddhist monasteries and temples. This image is a representation of the role assumed by Manjusri as an aide to the Buddha in teaching the Dharma. It implies that although Manjusri has the outward appearance of a bhiksu, he in fact is an accomplished bodhisattva. Another common portrayal is the "Manjusri of the five hair buns," which symbolizes the five kinds of wisdom[14] and the five Buddhas[15] to show that, while the Bodhisattva is presented in the form of a child, he actually possesses the wisdom of all Buddhas.

It is recorded in the sutras that Manjusri Bodhisattva has exceptional wisdom and is brilliant in rhetoric. During the Buddha's forty-nine years of teaching the Dharma in over three

[11] The lion is an important Buddhist symbol. The Buddha is the greatest among all human beings just as the lion is the king of all animals, and as such the lion is an image frequently used to express the Buddha's fearlessness and greatness. When sound of the Buddha teaching is called the "lion's roar," and the place where the Buddha sits is called a "lion throne."

[12] Peacocks are auspicious birds with a grand appearance and beautiful colors. Riding on a peacock symbolizes turning the Dharma Wheel.

[13] Located in the northeast part of Shanxi Province.

[14] The wisdom of the Buddha, incredible wisdom, indescribable wisdom, great and wide wisdom, and supreme wisdom.

[15] Vairocana, Aksobhya, Ratnasambhava, Amitabha, and Amoghasiddhi.

hundred assemblies, Manjusri was present in almost all of them. For example, in the *Vimalakirti Sutra*, it is stated that, when none of the arhats or bodhisattvas would dare to call upon the bedridden Upasaka Vimalakirti, Manjusri came forward to lead them there and took the opportunity to have a lively debate with Vimalakirti on the subject of non-duality. This event was a good illustration of Manjusri's wisdom, nobility and virtue.

The *Lotus Sutra* says that when the Buddha emitted rays of light from the tuft of white hair between his eyebrows during the assembly at Vulture Peak, Manjusri fully understood the Buddha's intention and immediately implored the Buddha to teach the Dharma and to encourage all to accomplish the vehicle of Buddhahood. The implications of this sutra became the foundation of Mahayana teaching. Furthermore, due to the demonstration of Manjusri's wisdom and virtue at the above assembly, all other bodhisattvas and arhats sincerely venerated him as a great Dharma friend.

In the *Flower Ornament Sutra*, it is implied that Sudhana was encouraged by Manjusri to travel to the southern kingdom states to visit and study from the fifty-three sagely masters, marking the beginning of travel-study in Buddhism. In the *Surangama Sutra*, it was also Manjusri Bodhisattva who rescued Ananda from the seduction of Lady Matangi. The part played by Manjusri in this incident fully demonstrates the Bodhisattva's crucial role in helping to prevent novices from deviating from the proper course of cultivation.

It is stated in the *Sutra on the Parinirvana of Manjusri* that one night, while the Buddha was meditating in the Jetavana Vihara, he radiated a brilliant light that brightened up the room of Manjusri Bodhisattva. Sariputra knew instantly that this show of supernatural power signaled the Buddha's imminent delivery of wondrous Dharma to benefit sentient beings. Without delay, he ordered Ananda to call an assembly of all the bhiksus. In reply to a query raised by Bhadrapala during the assembly, the Buddha described the loving kindness and great compassion of Manjusri Bodhisattva. He related how the Bodhisattva, having renounced the household life to practice the Way of the Buddha, constantly abided in the *Surangama-samadhi*, and confirmed that Manjusri Bodhisattva possessed infinite supernatural powers and myriad manifestations. Any sentient being that hears of the name of Manjusri Bodhisattva gets rid of all the unwholesomeness of twelve billion kalpas, and those who pay homage to the Bodhisattva are to be born into Buddhist families and be protected by the mighty power of the Bodhisattva in all future lives to come.

Manjusri Bodhisattva was skillful in expounding the Dharma, such that any difficulties that one encountered would suddenly be understood after his exposition of the Dharma. When delivering the Dharma, Manjusri Bodhisattva would employ frequent use of analogies, counter-questioning, evidentiary examples, negation and sharp wit to mentally stimulate the audience and guide them with skillful means. His unique style is well depicted in the *Sutra of King Ajatasatru.* Having committed patricide, one of the five great violations, King Ajatasatru was so haunted by his own wrongdoing that he was utterly filled with guilt and remorse. Later, he sought the Dharma from Manjusri in the hope that the Bodhisattva could help relieve his doubt and remorse. However, Manjusri told him that even if he had implored as many Buddhas as the grains of sand along the shore of the Ganges to find a solution to his problem, none would have been able to help him. Ajatasatru was so shocked to hear this that he fell off his seat. Manjusri had not meant to disappoint the king, but only wanted Ajatasatru to tackle the problem at its source; thus, he said to the king, "The Buddha is awakened to the truth that all phenomena are like infinite space and knows that their nature is originally pure and uncontaminated, and hence there is nothing to dispel."

Manjusri Bodhisattva continues to manifest in our midst, teaching the Dharma. Legend has it that Chan Master Wenxi[16] in the Tang dynasty received Dharma instructions from Manjusri when he went to visit Mount Wutai. When Wenxi later went to study with Chan Master Yangshan, he attained awakening. He then settled down to work as a cook. One day, amidst the steam from the rice cooker he again saw the manifestation of Manjusri. Wenxi then raised a wooden rice spoon, struck, and said, "Manjusri is Manjusri; Wenxi is Wenxi. You will not fool me today!" This shows that Master Wenxi had already attained the ability to clearly understand the truth of non-duality of the self and others. Another legend recorded in the Chronicle of Master Xuyun describes how Master Xuyun[17] had met twice with Manjusri Bodhisattva, manifesting as Elder Wenji, during his pilgrimage to Mount Wutai. In addition to saving his life from severe illness on both occasions, the Bodhisattva also expounded the Dharma to him, helping him to realize that paying homage to the Buddha lies only in the sincerity of one's heart.

Manjusri Bodhisattva is the Prince of the Dharma,
Manjusri Bodhisattva is the foremost of all bodhisattvas
and arhats,

[16] (821-900). He was a monk of the Weiyang School, carried on the teachings of Yangshan Huiji (840-916) and obtained enlightenment.
[17] (1840-1959), born in Hunan Province. After the establishment of the Republic of China, he continued the teachings of the Weiyang School, and single-handedly linked the circulation of the traditions of the Five Schools.

*Manjusri Bodhisattva is an example for every Buddhist
to follow,*
*Manjusri Bodhisattva is the pride and glory of
Buddhism,*
Manjusri Bodhisattva is the manifestation of wisdom,
*Manjusri Bodhisattva has truly realized the prajna
wisdom of emptiness,*
He is free of all afflictions,
Manjusri Bodhisattva is the manifestation of power,
*He can liberate sentient beings from suffering and
danger.*

Chapter Six

Samantabhadra

The Bodhisattva of Great Cultivation

Samantabhadra Bodhisattva is one of the three sages of the Avatamsaka realm[18] and is also known as the "King of Great Vows." He is also known as "Samantabhadra Sattva;" "Samantabhadra Mahasattva;" "Samantabhadra Tathagata;" and "the One of Universal Good." The Bodhisattva is the chief attendant to Vairocana Buddha, and also performs as a *Vajra Sattva* in assisting the Buddha and protecting the Dharma. According to the *Complete Enlightenment Sutra*, the word "*samanta*" means "the nature that pervades the universe," while "*bhadra*" means "the complete fulfillment of virtues based upon conditions." The *Record on Seeking the Profound Meanings of the Flower Ornament Sutra*[19] defines "*samanta*" as "the virtue that pervades all dharma realms," and "*bhadra*" as "the completeness of wisdom and fulfillment of goodness." On the other hand, the fifth Patriarch of the Huayan School, Master Zongmi, analyzed the meaning of "*Samantabhadra*" into three aspects:

---

[18] Vairocana Buddha, in the middle, is perfect in both wisdom and essence. Manjusri Bodhisattva, on the left, is perfect in wisdom. Samantabhadra Bodhisattva, on the right, is perfect in essence.

[19] *ch. Huayan Tanxun Ji.* Written by Fazang of the Tang Dynasty; it consists of twenty fascicles which describe the essence of the Flower Ornament Sutra. It describes the central teachings of the Huayan School.

1. The aspect of one's self-essence — "Samanta" means the nature that pervades all beings, while "bhadra" means the complete fulfillment of virtues based upon conditions.
2. The aspect of benefiting others — "Samanta" means helping all beings without exception, while "bhadra" means treating all beings well.
3. The aspect of being a ruler — "Samanta" means being a leader of virtue without any incompleteness, while "bhadra" means to mediate with benevolence and kind empathy.

Manjusri and Samantabhadra are often mentioned together, and images that include both Bodhisattvas have Manjusri on the back of a golden lion and Samantabhadra riding a white elephant with six tusks. While the former represents wisdom, insight and attainment, the latter is the manifestation of rationality, concentration and practice. This shows the equal importance of both understanding and cultivation. For example, when the young Sudhana traveled to visit the fifty-three sagely masters, his journey began with a visit to Manjusri, implying that one needs to enter the Way through wisdom. The last stop on his journey was to visit Samantabhadra, where Sudhana discovered from the Bodhisattva that cultivation is the means to attain the Way. The completion of Sudhana's journey also suggests the completion of the journey through wisdom and cultivation towards enlightenment. Thus there is a saying, "Manjusri is freely at ease with prajna wisdom; Samantabhadra is freely at ease with samadhi-concentration," implying that wisdom and concentration both exist as one.

During Samantabhadra Bodhisattva's past cultivation, he made ten great vows to practice to attain Buddhahood. These vows can be regarded as guidelines to cultivation for all practitioners of the bodhisattva path. The ten great vows are as follows:

1. Pay homage to all Buddhas — This vow is to have respect for all sentient beings. As all sentient beings have the same Buddha nature, they should be equally respected, as Sadaparibhuta Bodhisattva said, "I dare not denigrate any one of you, for you are all going to become Buddhas."

2. Praise the Tathagatas — This vow is to practice giving through speech and language. While it may be difficult to donate material possessions, one can speak out for righteous principles or share the Dharma with others, thereby demonstrating that giving through speech is easy to practice. During the Buddha's past cultivation, his practice of praising others led him to attain Buddhahood earlier than Maitreya Bodhisattva. This emphasizes the importance of this practice.

3. Practice offering extensively — This vow is to create good affinities with others. In practicing the Dharma, making offerings to parents, teachers, and the Triple Gem can be categorized into two,[20] three,[21] four,[22] and ten types of offerings.[23] Regardless of the type of offering, it remains the best method for forming good affinities and enhancing communication. Even in the Western Pure Land of Ultimate

---

[20] Stated as material goods and the Dharma in the *Treatise on the Ten Stages of the Bodhisattva*; and as the teachings of enlightenment and practice in the *Chapter on the Offerings of Vairocana Sutra*.

[21] Stated as material goods, the Dharma, and methods of contemplation in the *Annotation on the Chapter of the Great Vows of the Samantabhadra Bodhisattva*; as nourishment, worship, and deeds, in the *Treatise on the Ten Stages Sutra*; and as body, speech, and mind in the *Explanation on the Passages and Sentences of the Lotus Sutra*.

[22] Stated as flowers, joined palms, compassion, and thoughts in *Commentary and Explanation on the Vairocana Sutra*; as clothing, food, shelter, and medicine in the *Gradual Discourses of the Buddha*; and as banners, light, flowers, and incense in *Sutra on the Buddha of Infinite Life*.

[23] Stated as flowers, incense, garlands, incense powder, soap, burning incense, canopies, banners, clothing, and music in the *Lotus Sutra*; and as offerings of the body, articles of worship, offerings in the presence of the Buddha, offerings not in the presence of the Buddha, offerings made to others, offerings of material goods, the dedication of merit, not offering impure goods, and the offering of the utmost attainment in the *Sutra of Bodhisattva Stages*.

Bliss, offerings of clothing and flowers are made at the beginning of each day to the Buddhas of the ten directions.[24] Making offerings is thus seen as an essential part of cultivating the Buddha way.

4. Repent all unwholesome karma — This vow requires introspection in daily living.   In day-to-day activities, sentient beings often commit unintentional transgressions in their actions, speech and thoughts; it is only through the three kinds of repentance[25] that physical and mental purity can be restored.   Although Devadatta[26] had committed atrocious deeds in the Buddha's time, he was eventually redeemed because he truly repented.   Therefore, it is important to reflect and repent in our daily lives.

5. Rejoice in others' merits and virtues — This vow refers to the purity of intentions. A Buddhist practitioner should learn to nurture the seeds of merit in order to one day reap its harvest. However, to accumulate merit and virtue, we need to have pure and joyful intentions. Even the smallest deed of the body, mind or speech performed through a pure and joyful intention can bring boundless merit. An example of this is the act of Visakha,[27] who donated a garment embroidered with pearls out of joyful appreciation for the Dharma spoken by the Buddha. Her generous gesture subsequently led to the construction of a vihara for the sangha. Consequently, the merit and virtue from the spark of a pure and joyful intention can have remarkable results.

---

[24] As described in the *Amitabha Sutra*.

[25] Repentance through dharma ceremonies, visions of Buddhas and bodhisattvas, and understanding the emptiness of all phenomena.

[26] Cousin of the Buddha and brother of Ananda, he was often hostile to the Buddha and destroyed the peace and harmony of the sangha.

[27] Story as told in the *Sutra on the Treasury of Truth* (*Dharmapada*). Visakha is the daughter of an elder in the Anga Kingdom who, after studying with the Buddha, attained the fruit of the stream-entry (*srotapanna*).

6. Request the turning of the Dharma Wheel — This vow means to request the teaching of the truth. The Dharma is often allegorized as a vessel of liberation, hence the constant need to keep it in motion in order to liberate sentient beings from the sea of suffering. The turning of the Dharma Wheel first began when Elder Sudatta invited the Buddha to expound on the Dharma in Sravasti, which led to the dissemination of the Dharma throughout India.

7. Request the presence of Buddhas in the world — This vow is to be respectful and courteous to the sagely and virtuous. Requesting the presence of Buddhas in the world is extremely important. When the Buddha first attained enlightenment and was awakened to the truth of dependent origination in all phenomena, he was quite certain it was beyond the comprehension of ordinary people of this world. Had the Brahma King not implored the Buddha to stay and spread the Dharma he had realized he would have gone straight into nirvana. It was out of compassion for the sentient beings of this world that the Buddha began to disseminate his teachings, thus giving them an opportunity to see the illumination of the truth.

8. Always learn the Dharma — This is vow is to follow the wise. There is a saying, "Those who come near red will turn rosy; those who draw close to black will be darkened." The ten great disciples and the 1,250 great bhiksus followed the Buddha wherever he went, and it was not long before all of them attained the noble fruit of arhatship. This implies that it is important to follow the wise and to always learn the Dharma.

9. Forever assist according to sentient beings needs and abilites — This vow is to have regard for the viewpoints and needs

of sentient beings. The Buddha was very democratic in the way he handled daily affairs. Samantabhadra Bodhisattva and Prince Sudhana were the most aware of the Buddha's fair consideration of all views voiced in the community. Therefore, they are also foremost in respecting and not opposing the viewpoints and needs of sentient beings. This is the spirit behind the vow of always obliging the needs of sentient beings.

10. Dedicate merit and virtue to all sentient beings — This vow is to integrate all dharma realms. To achieve complete integration of all dharma realms, we should view others' interests as our own, understand the truth behind all issues, and consider the consequences of all actions. It is only then that we are able to turn impurity into purity, turn unwholesomeness into wholesomeness, turn unwholesome views into the right way, and transform arising and cessation into tranquility. The great vows of the Bodhisattva will only be accomplished when this goal is reached.

Samantabhadra Bodhisattva is the symbol of vows and practice in Mahayana Buddhism and a model practitioner on the bodhisattva path. Coupled with the wisdom of Manjusri, the two Bodhisattvas represent practice, vow and theory, which results in the complete and perfect Mahayana Buddha way.

Chapter Seven

Ksitigarbha

The Bodhisattva of Great Vows

"Not until hell is vacant shall I become a Buddha; only when all sentient beings are liberated will I attain bodhi." There is no better expression than this to depict the spirit of Ksitigarbha Bodhisattva.

Of the numerous great bodhisattvas, Avalokitesvara, Manjusri, Samantabhadra and Ksitigarbha represent compassion, wisdom, practice, and great vows respectively. The name Ksitigarbha or Earth Store conveys several meanings. The word "earth" means:

1. The Bodhisattva can nurture virtuous practices just as the earth can nurture everything.
2. The Bodhisattva can embrace all sentient beings just as the earth can hold a great deal.
3. The Bodhisattva can foster countless virtues and merits just as the earth can foster a myriad of things.

The word "store" means:

1. The Bodhisattva's hidden virtues, which are the *Dharma-kaya*, prajna wisdom, and liberation.[28]
2. The Bodhisattva's store of virtues that can offer endless benefits to sentient beings.
3. The Bodhisattva's ability to develop the treasury of potential within sentient beings.

"Earth" is a metaphor for the Bodhisattva's vast ability to foster, hold, store, support, embrace, and to be relied upon. It is also a representation of the Bodhisattva's vow, which is indestructible like a diamond (*vajra*) and unwavering like a massive rock. The word "store" also implies that the Bodhisattva is like a "hidden treasury" that holds limitless treasures which can be used to help the poor. Therefore, it also has the connotation of being hidden, tolerant, embracing and nurturing.

The *Sutra on the Fundamental Vows of the Earth Store Bodhisattva* (*Ksitigarbha Bodhisattva Pranidhana Sutra*) is a widely distributed and honored sutra in China. It tells of Ksitigarbha Bodhisattva as the son of an elder in a past life and describes how he resolved to cultivate to liberate all suffering sentient beings and help them attain enlightenment. According to the sutra, when Ksitigarbha became a king during one of his past lives, he made a great vow before the All-Wisdom-Accomplished Buddha (*Sarvajnasiddharta Tathagata*) to liberate all sentient beings from the unwholesome realm and to not forsake a single one.

---

[28] According to the *Summary of Mahayana Doctrine*, "Dharmakaya" refers to the suchness that is inherent in all sentient beings or to the body that is complete in virtue and merit. "Liberation" is leaving the bonds of suffering and affliction. "Prajna wisdom" is the wisdom of enlightenment. Dharmakaya, liberation, and prajna wisdom are known as the three virtues of the Buddha, or as the three aspects of Buddha nature.

The sutra also gives an account of the Bodhisattva's benevolent deeds and filial piety in past lives. For instance, when Ksitigarbha was a Brahman girl in one life, she invoked the Enlightenment-Flower-Samadhi-At-Ease Buddha to bestow faith in the Triple Gem upon her parents so that they might find liberation. In another life when the Bodhisattva was Lady Bright Eye (*Prabhacaksuh*), she made offerings to an arhat in the hope that this could save her mother from the torments of hell. As a result, Ksitigarbha Bodhisattva's resolve in filial piety is exemplary for all Buddhist practitioners.

The sutra also states that when the Buddha saw an opportunity to liberate his mother, Queen Maya, he left for Tusita Heaven, where he spent three months expounding on the *Sutra on the Fundamental Vows of the Earth Store Bodhisattva* and extolled the merits of Ksitigarbha to his mother. It is for this reason that the sutra came to be known in Buddhism as the sutra on filial piety.

In the *Sutra on the Fundamental Vows of the Earth Store Bodhisattva*, much emphasis is placed on the countless indescribable attributes of Ksitigarbha Bodhisattva, including his supernatural powers, compassion, wisdom, eloquence and concentration. It is said that even the name of the sutra itself is endowed with inconceivable power. For these reasons, Ksitigarbha Bodhisattva is acknowledged as an inconceivable sage.

The greatness of Ksitigarbha's vow and inspiration is demonstrated through the Bodhisattva's commitment to benefit all sentient beings and widely teach the Dharma according to conditions. To quote from the *Sutra on the Fundamental Vows of the Earth Store Bodhisattva*:

"...to those who kill, Ksitigarbha Bodhisattva speaks of the retribution of misfortune and premature death; to those who

steal, the retribution of poverty and suffering; to those who commit sexual misconduct, the retribution of rebirth as sparrows, pigeons or mandarin ducks; to those who use harsh words, the retribution of quarrels and fights in the family; to those who slander, the retribution of a tongue-less or ulcerous mouth; to those full of hatred and resentment, the retribution of ugliness and physical deformation; to those who are stingy and miserly, the retribution of disappointment in what they want; to gluttons of food and drink, the retribution of thirst, hunger and throat diseases; to those who indulge in hunting, the retribution of death in fear and insanity; to those who are against their parents, the retribution of death in natural disasters; to those who commit arson in the forests, the retribution of death through delirium; to abusive parents or step-parents, the retribution of being abused themselves in future lifetimes; to those who catch or trap the young or newly born, the retribution of separation from one's children or parents; to those who slander the Triple Gem, the retribution of being blind, deaf and mute; to those who slight the Dharma or regard the teachings with arrogance, the retribution of dwelling permanently in the lower realms; to those who abuse the property of the sangha, the retribution of rebirth in hell for a billion kalpas; to those who falsely accuse or defile members of the sangha, the retribution of being born as animals; to those who harm lives by boiling, burning, cutting and chopping, the retribution of repayment in kind; to those who violate the precepts and purity, the retribution of being starving beasts; to those who break things unreasonably, the retribution of deficiency and not obtaining what they want; to those who are arrogant and haughty, the retribution of becoming lowly; to those who are double-tongued in causing dissension, the

retribution of having no tongue, or a hundred tongues; to those
with heretical or wrong views, the retribution of being born on
the border."[29]

By the strength of his great vow, Ksitigarbha Bodhisattva
has liberated numerous sentient beings in his many lives.
However, the Bodhisattva's great vow, "Not until hell is vacant
shall I become a Buddha," is often misinterpreted as he will
never attain Buddhahood. In the Bodhisattva's mind, hell is
already empty.

Ksitigarbha Bodhisattva was present at many of the
Buddha's Dharma assemblies. It is also believed that the
Bodhisattva once manifested as Prince Jin Qiaojue of Korea, who
traveled to Mount Jiuhua in Anhui, China, and liberated the
wealthy Mr. Ming and his son. Later, the prince remained on
Mount Jiuhua to cultivate the Dharma. On one occasion, the
prince recited a poem to comfort his homesick attendant:

> *In the lonely monastery, you missed your home;*
> *Bid farewell to Mount Jiuhua, then, and leave the house*
>   *in the clouds.*
> *You loved to ride a bamboo hobby horse along the*
>   *bamboo fence;*
> *In this golden dharma ground, you neglected to*
>   *accumulate merits.*
> *While gathering water from the stream, try not to reach*
>   *for the moon;*
> *You will enjoy making tea and arranging flowers.*
> *Leave, not to worry, you must not shed tears;*
> *This old monk has the company of the mist and the*
>   *clouds.*

---

[29] The place where one cannot hear and learn the Dharma.

Ksitigarbha is a hospitable bodhisattva. There are many records of the Bodhisattva's manifestations such as those reported in the deeds of his past cultivation, in historical events, and in stories in both the past and modern times. Furthermore, among the great bodhisattvas, Ksitigarbha is the only one who has appeared as a bhiksu. A common portrayal of the Bodhisattva is one in which he is holding a scepter in the right hand and a pearl in the left. This dignified image of the Bodhisattva has inspired many devotees.

CHAPTER EIGHT

Maitreya

The Bodhisattva of Joy

Up in the heavens or down below,
there is nothing comparable to the Buddha,
Even the worlds of the ten directions cannot compare.
I have seen everything that this universe can offer,
Yet nothing can match the Buddha.

This praising gatha was recited by Sakyamuni at the time when he and Maitreya were both learning under the guidance of Tisya Buddha.[30] Because Sakyamuni had practiced an additional Dharma method, that of praising the Buddhas, and recited the above gatha, he attained Buddhahood before Maitreya. Therefore, Maitreya is called the "Bodhisattva to succeed Sakyamuni as the next future Buddha;"[31] when he will descend to earth he will then attain Buddhahood.

Born in Varanasi, India, Maitreya Bodhisattva was originally given a name that means "loving kindness." However, he was

---

[30] When the Buddha was cultivating thirty-two marks of excellence and eighty noble qualities he encountered Tisya Buddha.

[31] This means that after this life, the Bodhisattva will be reborn in this world and become a Buddha. Preceding his Buddhahood, he is known as the Bodhisattva of Equal Enlightenment (*ekajatipratibaddha*).

later also known as Ajita. Initially, Maitreya practiced under his uncle's guidance. Later, he became a disciple of the Buddha. After Maitreya realized the truth, the Buddha foretold of Maitreya's attainment of Buddhahood in this world. Maitreya will descend from Tusita Heaven and hold three assemblies to teach the Dharma following his enlightenment under the *nagapuspa* tree.[32]

One characteristic of Maitreya's cultivation is that he "did not practice to attain meditative concentration, nor did he sever afflictions." His vow was to consistently practice giving charity, offering compassion and loving kindness to all, upholding the precepts, and contemplating introspectively for wisdom. In other words, his primary concern was not for his own liberation from birth and death but for the benefit of others.

The *Sutra on the Ascent of Maitreya*,[33] the *Sutra on the Descent of Maitreya*,[34] and the *Sutra on Maitreya's Great*

---

[32] 5.67 billion years after Sakyamuni's parinirvana, Maitreya will descend from Tusita Heaven to earth and become a Buddha. Upon attaining Buddhahood, he will hold three turnings of the Dharma Wheel. According to the sutra, at Maitreya's first turning of the Dharma Wheel, he will liberate 9.6 billion sentient beings who uphold the Five Precepts. At his second turning, he will liberate 9.4 billion sentient beings who take refuge in the Triple Gem. At his third and last turning, he will liberate 9.2 billion sentient beings who recite the name of a Buddha.

[33] The complete name of this sutra is the *Sutra on the Contemplation of Maitreya's Ascent to Tusita Heaven*. It is also known as the *Sutra on Maitreya Bodhisattva's Parinirvana*, the *Sutra on the Contemplation of Maitreya's Ascent*, the *Sutra on the Contemplation of Maitreya* and the *Sutra on the Ascent*. This sutra consists of only one fascicle. It was translated by Juqu Jingsheng (?-464 BCE) in the Liu Song Dynasty. Among the sutras on Maitreya, this was the last to be developed. It is also one of the most important sutras for practitioners of the Pure Land of Maitreya.

[34] This sutra is also known as the *Sutra on the Contemplation of Maitreya Bodhisattva's Descent*, the *Sutra on the Contemplation of Maitreya's Descent*, the *Sutra on Maitreya's Next to Come* and the *Sutra of Descent*. This sutra consists of only one fascicle and was translated by Dharmaraksa during the Western Jin Dynasty.

Achievement,[35] are collectively known as The Three Sutras on Maitreya. The *Sutra on the Ascent of Maitreya* is mainly a narration of events leading to Maitreya's ascension to Tusita Heaven[36] and his propagation of the Dharma in the Inner Palace of Tusita. The *Sutra on the Descent of Maitreya* is about the future, and describes how Maitreya is going to descend to this world from Tusita Heaven to attain Buddhahood, teach the Dharma and liberate sentient beings of this world.

The original image of Maitreya portrays him as wearing a jeweled crown and dressed in heavenly attire adorned with jewels. He would either be sitting crossed-legged or seated with one leg naturally hanging to the ground, in a posture of deep thinking, with one hand on his cheek. Today, however, the most common image of Maitreya is that of a monk with a laughing face, large ears and a potbelly, sitting bare-chested in a casual posture. This is in fact the portrayal of the manifestation of Maitreya as a monk called Budai[37] in the Liang Period of the Five Dynasties in China. As he traveled along and taught the Dharma, he was heard reciting the following verse: "Maitreya, the true Maitreya, transformed in a million forms, Appearing to all at all times, and yet no one knows me at all."

There is another popular ballad about Maitreya that he wrote to describe himself:

---

[35] Also known as the *Sutra on Maitreya Becoming a Buddha*, the sutra consists of one fascicle and was translated by Kumarajiva during the Yao Qin Dynasty. Among the sutras on Maitreya, this is the most complete. It contains a dialogue between Sariputra and Sakyamuni Buddha where Sariputra asks about what the state of the world will be when Maitreya arrives.

[36] Literally, "Heaven of Satisfaction," "Heaven of Contentment," or "Heaven of Joy." The fourth of the six heavens in the desire realm. This heaven and Yama heaven are called Tuya.

[37] A monk from the Liang Period of the Five Dynasties, Budai was said to be a manifestation of Maitreya Bodhisattva. He was often seen carrying a sack on his shoulder.

An old dolt wears a monk's robe;
plain rice can fill his belly.
When the robe is torn and tethered,
he'll patch it to weather the cold.
He lets all things resolve according to conditions.
If someone scolds the old dolt,
the old dolt will only say "fine;"
When someone beats him up,
he will lie down for a snooze;
When he is spat on in the face,
he will simply leave it to dry;
"This will save me the trouble,
while the person will have no more grudges."
This is a true perfection, and a wondrous treasure;
If this is really understood,
why should one worry that one cannot get on the Path?
No argument over what's right and wrong,
no home to be concerned about,
No fight about whether it's yours or mine,
no need to be the hero.
Out of the burning trench he jumps,
to become pure and cool,
Enlightened to the truth of longevity,
he walks on in the company of the sun and moon.

Today, the happy image of Maitreya can be found at the main entrance to every monastery, and even ordinary people know him as the Happy Buddha. There are usually two couplets hanging beside his image, which read: "The large belly can hold the myriad things of this world; the smile is always there to laugh away the misery of all time."

In every temple and monastery, there is usually also a statue of Maitreya as Budai at the center of the dining hall. For example, in the dining hall at Tiantong Temple, Zhejiang, China, there is a verse which hangs beside the statue of Maitreya that reads:

Displaying poverty,
Maitreya takes the seat of the host in the dining hall;
His ear stretches but he remains unmoved
When the disciplinary officer pulls his ear.
The hosting master shows magnanimity,
Joyfully inviting Maitreya to stay;
He orders the attendants to add another seat,
And the seat of the host is moved.

During the Eastern Jin Dynasty, Fu Jian once gave a statue of Maitreya to Master Daoan[38] as a gift. This gesture later influenced Master Daoan and his disciples, Fayu, Fuseng and Tanjie to make the vow to be reborn in Maitreya's Inner Palace of Tusita Heaven. Since then, many great Chinese masters such as Master Xuanzang in the Tang Dynasty, Master Taixu, Master Cihang[39] and Venerable Haolin[40] became believers in the Maitreya Pure Land and vowed to be reborn there.

What makes the Pure Land of Maitreya distinctive is that, unlike the other Pure Lands, it is not as distant from the Saha

---

[38] Master Daoan (312-385) or (314-385) was born during the Eastern Jin Dynasty, joined the monastic order at age of twelve and taught the Dharma in Hubei for fifteen years. He then devoted his life to translating the Buddhist sutras and played a critical role in Eastern Jin Buddhism. He also established "Shi" as the surname for monastics.
[39] Master Cihang (1895-1954) was born in Fujian. Famously his physical body remained undecayed after three years of being buried in an urn seated in a meditation posture. His posthumous writings were published as the *Collections of Master Cihang*.
[40] Born in 1927 in the city of Hefei in Anhui Province.

world. Tusita heaven is still within the realm of sensual desires, and those who resolve to be reborn there are not required either to have been ordained or to have attained the state of concentrated mindfulness. They need only uphold the Five Precepts, frequently practice the Eight Precepts of Purification, and do good deeds to accrue merit. Hence, cultivation for rebirth in Maitreya's Pure Land is sometimes considered much easier to accomplish and more suited to the inclinations of people in the modern world.

Although Maitreya's Pure Land is a dharma realm of equality and wholesomeness suitable for all sentient beings, there are some skeptics who question the possibility of attaining full liberation in the Pure Land that is within the realm of sensual desires. Actually, if one resides in the Pure Land of Maitreya and is always listening and learning the Dharma, how could one then be trapped in the transmigration of birth and death?

Unfortunately, certain cults that exploit the image of Maitreya Bodhisattva have sprouted up. They advocate that the era of Sakyamuni Buddha has ended and that Maitreya Buddha is the present "Buddha in charge." Behind the façade of these pseudo-Buddhist teachings, they run illegal societies and syndicates to deceive the general public, both spiritually and financially. However, it was explicitly stated in the sutras that Maitreya would only attain Buddhahood under the *nagapuspa* tree 5,670 million years after Sakyamuni Buddha, to widely liberate sentient beings.

Faith in Maitreya Bodhisattva is usually inspired by the various benefits that accompany rebirth within the Inner Palace of Tusita Heaven. What is often overlooked, however, is the Bodhisattva's emphasis on the development of a pure land in this world, here and now. There is a passage in the *Sutra on the Descent of Maitreya* that describes the world when Maitreya descends to it. It says that this world will be an expanse of brightness, with the earth as smooth and flat as a mirror, covered in green pastures. There, flowers will be scented and in full bloom, and the climate during the four seasons most pleasant. There will be a plentiful harvest and hence no need to hoard or possess. Every necessity will be readily available, and everyone will live in harmony with one another. They will treat each other with loving kindness, and there will be no wars or conflicts. With peace and security everywhere, there will be true happiness for all. This is the picture of a pure land that encompasses purity, goodness and beauty. Perhaps it is more important to start working towards the realization of this Pure Land in preparation for the arrival of Maitreya Bodhisattva!

CHAPTER NINE

Asvaghosa
The Artist

"It is people that propagate the Way, not the Way that propagates people." The truth of this saying accurately depicts the contributions made by Asvaghosa Bodhisattva to the transmission of Buddhism.

Born into a Brahman family from Sravasti in Central India in the 2nd Century CE, Asvaghosa Bodhisattva was initially a heretic practitioner of extensive knowledge. Later, he studied under Elder Parsva and took refuge as his follower. Once ordained , Asvaghosa delved into the study of Buddhism, and on attaining a profound understanding of the Tripitaka he began to propagate the Dharma. Mahayana Buddhism, which he advocated, soon became widely accepted and was predominant all over India.

Asvaghosa was distinguished in both Buddhist literature and music. He composed poetry, dramas and music, all of which were of prominence at the time. Written in Sanskrit, *Verses on the Deeds of the Buddha* (*Buddhacarita*)[41] is a collection of narrative poetry

---

[41] T. vol. 4, no. 192. Consists of five fascicles with a total of twenty-eight chapters. Translated by Dharmaraksa, it describes the life of the Buddha from his birth to the distribution of his relics upon his parinirvana. It is Asvaghosa's most famous work and is a monumental achievement of ancient Indian literature.

that is beautifully expressed, intricately descriptive and lively in style. It is an innovative form of aesthetic writing and ranked as an ingenious piece of classical Sanskrit literature. The book was so popular in ancient India and South East Asia, that by the time of the Kusana Kingdom,[42] many sculptures were based on the contents of this collection of poetry. Together with *The Saundarananda Poetry* (*Saundarananda-kavya*), they are the two most important works by Asvaghosa Bodhisattva.

With regard to music, the songs Asvaghosa Bodhisattva wrote for the drama, *The Story of Rastrapala*,[43] were a revelation on worldly impermanence and suffering. When performed in the city of Pataliputra, the lyrics so touched the audience of five hundred princes that they subsequently decided to be ordained and cultivate the Buddha way. This became a notable incident in Buddhist history as it is a perfect example of teaching Dharma to sentient beings through music. At the beginning of the twentieth century, frayed manuscripts of three ancient Indian plays were recovered in Xinjiang China. One of these, *The Life of Sariputra* (*Sariputra-prakarana*), is another original work of Asvaghosa, which is now deemed the oldest Sanskrit play.

Spreading the Dharma through music and various forms of literary compositions had become the main undertakings of Asvaghosa Bodhisattva, and his reputation traveled far and

---

[42] Kusana existed between the end of the 1st Century CE and mid-3rd Century CE. The empire was located in the northwestern part of India between Central Asia and Iran. It is believed to be the largest empire after King Asoka's. Under its reign, trade was conducted between the Roman Empire and China. The Kusana Kingdom was well-known for its Gandharan art and the teachings of the Sarvastivadin School.

[43] Rastrapala was born in a wealthy family, in a village called Thullakotthita in the state of Kuru. He was ordained and practiced under Sakyamuni Buddha. Later, when he returned to his village, his parents tried to lure him away from his monastic vows by distracting him with a woman. However, the woman was so moved by his instructions on the Dharma that she became a nun. Later, Asvaghosa adapted Rastrapala's story into a drama, and personally performed the drama in Pataliputra.

wide. In fact, King Kaniska[44] of the Kusana Kingdom was so impressed by the work of Asvaghosa that when he invaded Magadha, he demanded the Buddha's alms bowl and Asvaghosa in lieu of his original demand for a great amount of gold as the condition for withdrawing his attacking troops. After Asvaghosa was delivered to King Kaniska, he began teaching the Dharma to the King, and was later honored as the kingdom's National Master. Besides learning the Dharma from Asvaghosa, the King also ordered the construction of many stupas, monasteries and Buddhist structures throughout his kingdom. These later became known in the history of Buddhist art as Gandharan Art.

Since the conversion of King Kaniska to Buddhism, the discord in doctrinal views held by different Buddhist schools had reached a point where the average practitioner found it confusing to know which path to follow. Considering this to be a major obstacle in the development of Buddhism, the king invited the Elder Parsva to gather an assembly of the most virtuous people to compile and reconcile these differences.

Five hundred arhats and five hundred bodhisattvas took part in this assembly held in Kashmir. They concluded that all the eighteen schools offer the same teachings as the Buddha's teachings, and that the different schools exist to provide various Dharmas to guide the cultivation of people with different capabilities. This resolution finally brought an end to the schism within the Buddhist community that had existed for almost a hundred years. During the assembly, the participants also transferred the vinaya and several sutras that had been passed down in oral form into the written form for the first time,

---

[44] A member of the third generation in a line of kings of Kusana. Through inheritance and conquest, his kingdom extended from Central Asia to Central India. As a patron of Buddhism, he convened the Fourth Buddhist Council in Kashmir. King Kaniska and King Asoka are regarded as the two great protector kings of Buddhism.

revised numerous sutras that had been written previously, and finally annotated the Buddhist Canon. Asvaghosa Bodhisattva was elected as chief editor, and this assembly is now known in Buddhist history as the Fourth Council.[45]

While in northern India, Asvaghosa widely propagated Mahayana Buddhism and was lauded with the name "The Sun of Virtues." Furthermore, Asvaghosa's most important contribution was his documentation of numerous treatises and commentaries on the Buddhist teachings that challenged those with wrong views with the correct Dharma, leading them to a better understanding of the Buddhist teachings. According to the last section of the *Mahamaya Sutra*, "Six hundred years after the Buddha's parinirvana, ninety-six heretical views will thrive and destroy the Buddhist teachings. There will be a bhiksu named Asvaghosa, who, being excellent in expounding the Dharma, will subdue all the heretics of the various paths." In the Tibetan work the *Biography of Asvaghosa*, the Bodhisattva is described as one who "did not have a question he could not answer, or a polemic challenge he could not conquer. Just as a withered branch is blown off by gales, his contenders were frequently defeated with conviction." For this reason, Asvaghosa Bodhisattva was also revered for his eloquence and was called "the eloquent bhiksu."

In bringing Buddhist teachings into music, plays and poetry, Asvaghosa Bodhisattva had enriched the repertoire of Buddhist music. Among the treatises written by the Bodhisattva, the most important include the *Treatise on the Vyuharaja Sutra* and the

---

[45] Elder Parsva initiated the Fourth Council, Vasumitra was the head facilitator, and King Kaniska was the main sponsor. During the council the Tripitaka was revised and annotated, with one thousand verses of annotation each for the *sutras*, *vinaya*, and *sastras*. The collection of these annotations is known as the *Abhidharmamahavibhasa Sastra*.

Treatise on Awakening of Faith in Mahayana. The *Treatise on Awakening of Faith in Mahayana* places emphasis on the levels of practice in Mahayana cultivation such as one-mindedness, the two gates, the three greatnesses, the four faiths, and the five practices.[46] By understanding the treatise's teachings through wisdom and by putting them into practice we can depart from the cycle of birth and death and realize the state of suchness and nirvana. The *Treatise on Awakening of Faith in Mahayana* had since become a principal work of reference for several main Buddhist schools such as the Tiantai, Huayan, Chan, Pure Land and Esoteric schools.

Throughout his life, Asvaghosa Bodhisattva had skillfully employed musical and literary works to help disseminate the Buddhist teachings on the truth of impermanence, emptiness and suffering. He played a major role in the Fourth Council, which brought an end to the disputes among the different schools which had lasted for nearly a century. His *Treatise on Awakening of Faith in Mahayana* had reinforced the foundation of Mahayana Buddhism and enhanced the literature of Buddhism in general. He is highly esteemed in China, and was hailed as "The Buddha of Great Brightness and Illumination" for being both an outstanding Patriarch of the Western Regions, and as an accomplished pioneer of using music and art as a means of spreading Buddhism, the influence of which has proved to be far reaching and invaluable.

---

[46] "One-mindedness" is being one with suchness. The "two gates" are the gate to suchness and the gate to *samsara*. The "three greatnesses" are essence, form and application. The "four faiths" include faith in suchness and faith in the Buddha, Dharma, and Sangha. The "five practices" are giving, upholding precepts, patience, diligence, and stopping delusion and seeing the truth.

CHAPTER TEN

Nagarjuna

The Patriarch of Eight Schools

Of all the historical masters who specialized in the study of the sutras, sastras (treatises and commentaries), vinaya (precepts), and Chan, Nagarjuna is the only one lauded with both the title of "Master of a Thousand Sastras" and "Common Patriarch of Eight Schools."

Nagarjuna Bodhisattva was born between seven and eight hundred years after the Buddha's parinirvana in the kingdom of Vedali in Southern India. A prodigious child of Brahman descent he was gifted in all skills and had thorough knowledge of the Vedas[47] from a very young age. As a youth, Nagarjuna went to learn invisibility with three of his friends. Thereafter, the gang would secretly access the king's palace and indulge in the fun and pleasure of sexual misconduct with the ladies of the king's court. These pursuits soon landed them in trouble with the king's guards, and his friends lost their lives. Although Nagarjuna managed a fortuitous escape, he realized that desire was the source of suffering. Once Nagarjuna had resolved to be liberated from the bonds of desire, he made a trip to the

---

[47] The basic scriptures of Brahmanism. *"Veda"* means wisdom, knowledge, wisdom of knowledge, and knowledge of liberation.

Buddha's stupa where he renounced and was then ordained.

The now awakened Nagarjuna spent ninety days reading through all the sutras in the stupas, and although he understood the general meaning conveyed in each, he still had certain doubts. On his way to the Himalayas to seek advice from the sages of the time, he met an old bhiksu who gave him the *Mahayana Sutras*. Later he was also given a large number of *Vaipulya Sutras*[48] when he visited the palace of the Dragon clan in Southern India. Within ninety days, Nagarjuna made a major breakthrough in his spiritual cultivation and attained patience regarding the non-arising of dharmas.[49]

On leaving the Dragon palace, Nagarjuna traveled throughout India to propagate the Dharma. Along the way, he had several encounters with heretics in southern India, and an intense exchange of supernatural powers was performed between them. In the end, the prowess of Nagarjuna won over the heretics, and they were converted to Buddhism. In his attempt to proselytize to the King of Kosala in Central India, Nagarjuna enlisted himself in the king's army for seven years, serving voluntarily and without pay. During this time, he fully demonstrated his abilities by offering sagacious suggestions on military strategy. When Nagarjuna finally secured the chance to meet the king, a series of debates ensued. The king eventually submitted to the Dharma and subsequently came to be known as the "benevolent patron king of the Dharma." With the king's support, Nagarjuna became even more active in the propagation of the Dharma. Not only did he widely annotate the Mahayana

[48] *Vaipulya* refers to the Mahayana discourses of the Buddha. They explore the broad, profound, and universal Mahayana teachings and are distinctive from the Hinayana sutras.
[49] This refers to observing the principle of arising and cessation in all dharmas and developing patience for it. This understanding causes the mind to become settled, without stirring or moving.

sutras, but he also systematized the teaching of Mahayana Buddhism, enabling the Mahayana concept of prajna wisdom and the nature of emptiness to be spread across the whole of India.

Nagarjuna was a prolific writer of treatises on Buddhist doctrines and earned the title of "Master of a Thousand Sastras." Among his works, the *Treatise of the Perfection of Great Wisdom* (*Mahaprajnaparamita Sastra*), the *Treatise on the Middle Way* (*Madhyamika Sastra*) and the *Treatise on the Ten Stages of Bodhisattva* are the most important. The *Treatise on the Middle Way* (*Madhyamika Sastra*) elucidates the profound meaning of the nature of emptiness due to dependent origination. This work aims to show the way to liberation from the cycle of birth and death, and is used by practitioners of the three vehicles. The *Treatise of the Perfection of Great Wisdom* (*Mahaprajnaparamita Sastra*) explains the *Sutra of Prajna Wisdom*, and the *Treatise on the Ten Stages of Bodhisattva* is an attempt to interpret the *Chapter on the Ten Stages* in the *Flower Ornament Sutra* (*Avatamsaka Sutra*), adopting an esoteric approach to explain the magnanimous practice of the bodhisattvas.

One of Nagarjuna's works is the *Verses of Exhortation to the King*, a compendium of letters written by Nagarjuna to the King of Kosala designed to inspire the king to have faith in the Triple Gem and to support Buddhism. Many of these were written in the form of poems and, like the gathas in the *Sutra on the Treasury of Truth* (*Dharmapada*) that combine beautiful language with subtle meaning, they became very popular among the people. According to the *Journey to the South Sea to Convey and Take Refuge in Buddhism* (ch. *Nanhai Jigui Neifa Zhuan*), Master Yijing of China personally witnessed children reciting these poems and adults using them for daily reference when he was in India. Another work worth mentioning is the *Treatise to King Satavadana*, which was written especially for kings and rulers. It expounds on the way to rule a country and the relevance of the Buddhist faith. This is an important work that is reflective of Nagarjuna's view on politics from a Mahayana perspective.

Although very few of the Sanskrit versions of Nagarjuna's works exist today, many of them are extant in Tibetan translation. As Nagarjuna is considered a Patriarch of Esoteric Buddhism in Tibet, about one hundred of his works are included in the Tibetan Tripitaka, and these serve as a valuable source of material for research into Nagarjuna's thoughts. His *Treatise on the Middle Way* (*Madhyamika-sastra*), which advocates the study of emptiness, was a direct influence on the subsequent formation of the Middle Way School (*Madhyamaka School*). As such, Nagarjuna is regarded as the founding Patriarch of this School and also proclaimed the thirteenth Patriarch of the Chan School of the Handing Down of Sakyamuni's Teaching. Apart from being an important branch of Buddhist studies in Tibetan Buddhism, the ideas of the Middle Way School are fundamental to the doctrines of the Three Treatises School (ch. *Sanlun Zong*).[50] Nagarjuna well deserves the honor of "Master of Eight Schools," for the teachings of many Buddhist schools, including the Tiantai School,[51] have stemmed from his thought.

Nagarjuna taught at the University of Nalanda and later became its head. While he was in office there, the region was

---

[50] This school is based on Nagarjuna's *Treatise on the Middle Way, Treatise of the Twelve Aspects* and Aryadeva's *Treatise in a Hundred Verses*. It continues Nagarjuna's understanding of dependent origination.

[51] Founded by the Great Master Zhizhe during the Sui Dynasty, whose thoughts carried on those of Huisi of the Nanyue and Huiwen of the Northern Qi. Though this school originated in China, its doctrine can be traced back to Nagarjuna.

flooded due to its proximity to the Ganges. In the face of this emergency, Nagarjuna personally designed and organized the construction of a dam to mitigate further damage to the area. He was also responsible for opening up a canal that henceforth facilitated the trading of goods between the different kingdoms along its course. Nagarjuna demonstrated himself to be a capable engineer, and his involvement in these secular matters only proved him to be a true practitioner of the bodhisattva path.

To sum up his life, Nagarjuna was originally a scholar of Southern India who went north into the Himalayas before he was ordained in the Sarvastivadin School.[52] Having traveled all over India to propagate the Dharma, he returned to Kosala in Southern India. Nagarjuna's extensive knowledge and widespread teaching of Buddhism made him the master of Mahayana treatises. His exposition of the Middle Way in the *Treatise on the Middle Way* (*Madhyamika-sastra*) totally demolished the extreme heretical view of clinging to either non-existence or existence, when neither is the truth. This concept was crucial to the identification of Mahayana thought as distinct from the Hinayana, and it is in this respect that Nagarjuna's contribution to Mahayana Buddhism is considered to be as important as that of Asvaghosa, though he was the first to promote Mahayana Buddhism. It would certainly not be an overstatement to say that Nagarjuna Bodhisattva is foremost among practitioners of Mahayana Buddhism.

[52] The first schism formed among the Theravadan Schools. The doctrine of the Sarvastivadin School is the most representatived in the Theravadan School, which has passed down most of its written works. It was the most influential school in northern India and gradually moved south into central India and Sri Lanka, and became mainstream Buddhism. The Buddhism of Sri Lanka is the most representative of the Theravada School after the decline of the Theravada in India.

Significant Works of Nagarjuna:

> *Treatise of the Perfection of Great Wisdom*
>   *(Mahaprajnaparamita Sastra)*
> *Treatise on the Middle Way (Madhyamika-sastra)*
> *Treatise of the Twelve Aspects (Dvadasamukha-sastra)*
> *Seventy Discourses on Practicing Emptiness*
> *Treatise on Turning Disputes*
> *Treatise on the Ten Verses on the Truth*
> *Treatise on the Mahayana Refutation of Existence*
> *Treatise on the Ten Stages of Bodhisattva*
> *Treatise on the Mahayana Twenty Verses*
> *Treatise on Resources of Bodhi*
> *Treatise on the Precious, Correct Conduct of the King*
> *Verses of Exhortation and Prohibition to the King.*

CHAPTER ELEVEN

Aryadeva

The Champion of the Right Dharma

If the essence of Mahayana Bodhisattva practice is represented by the phrase "The intention is not for security and happiness of the self, but for sentient beings to be rid of suffering," then the spirit of Aryadeva Bodhisattva is embodied in the statement "For the perpetuation of right Dharma, there is no regret even if demolishing heretical views and revealing the truth means death."

Aryadeva was born around the third century CE and was one of the early interpreters of the thoughts of the Madhyamaka or Middle Way School in India. As a direct disciple of Nagarjuna Bodhisattva, Aryadeva further developed Mahayana teachings by dedicating his whole life to the disproving of heretical views. His fervent efforts to uphold and propagate the right Dharma eventually led to his martyrdom. In giving up his own life to defend the truth, Aryadeva came to be regarded as a paragon of the bodhisattva spirit and a Dharma protector.

Aryadeva came from a Brahman family of Southern India and was ordained under the Vatsiputriyah School,[53] one of the

---

[53] One of the twenty Hinayana schools. The Vatsiputriyah School broke away from the Sarvastivadin School 300 years after the Buddha's parinirvana, and advocated a view of the self (*pudgala*) as the main entity in the cycle of birth and death. Years later, "*pudgala*" greatly influenced the Mahayana doctrine of the *tathagatagarbha*.

twenty divisions of the Hinayana School. Besides being well known for his intelligence, wide scope of knowledge, and exceptional eloquence, he was also noted to be fearless in his actions. He had once plucked the eyes out of the image of Mahesvara[54] in public before gouging out one of his own as recompense just to demonstrate the ordinariness and spiritlessness of the traditional god. Since then, he was known as Kanadeva, or the "one-eyed deva."

Immediately after hearing about Nagarjuna, Aryadeva went all the way from his homeland to the Auspicious Mountain in Kosala in hopes of debating with him. As Nagarjuna had also heard of Aryadeva's wisdom and wit, he ordered an attendant to bring in a bowl of water as a welcoming gesture. Without uttering a word, Aryadeva reacted by placing a needle in the water and watched it sink. Nagarjuna's bowl of water was meant to symbolize the completeness of Buddha nature within him, which, although full to the brim like the water in the bowl, was not spilt. Aryadeva's response showed his understanding that the Dharma is suchness, and thus the true realization of one is the thorough understanding of all. The needle that sank right through to the bottom of the bowl was analogous to Aryadeva's insight, which had reached the heart of the truth. At the end of this subtle exchange, Nagarjuna instantly praised the attainment of Aryadeva who, inspired by the great wisdom of Nagarjuna, became his student and studied the Mahayana teachings, becoming one of his most distinguished followers.

At that time, the popularity of the heretics in Central and Southern India restricted Buddhist activities. In fact, for twelve years, the use of gongs and bells was suspended in all Buddhist monasteries. Nagarjuna wanted to go there to teach the Dharma,

---

[54] The supreme Brahman god, regarded as lord of the universe.

but anticipating the hardships his Dharma master would endure during the journey, Aryadeva volunteered to go there on his behalf.

From the beginning, Aryadeva pronounced his preference for "not establishing his own school," aiming instead to only "demolish the teachings of the heretics" through outright criticism and dispute. He nullified the extremist belief in either "everything has existence" or "everything does not have existence," and ultimately dismissed even the belief in the concurrence of both. As a token of appreciation, a memorial stupa was erected by the people of Southern India to commemorate the work of Aryadeva in eradicating heretical views and reviving the Buddhist teachings. This stupa, named "the stupa of reinstating Dharma instruments," was still there when Master Xuanzang reached India on his journey to the West.

In his lifelong efforts to illuminate the truth, Aryadeva accomplished a great deal. One example of his success were his achievements upon arriving in Southern India. The king initially did not believe in Buddhism. Aryadeva believed that to convert the ordinary people, it would be necessary to first convert their ruler. He therefore joined the army when the opportunity arose and was recruited as a commanding general. With his wisdom and ability, Aryadeva soon won the respect and obedience of his soldiers. In their subsequent encounters, the King was very impressed by Aryadeva and was eventually converted to Buddhism, along with many heretics. Aryadeva advised the king on three things; "Of all the sagely and virtuous, the Buddha is the foremost; of all the teachings, that of the Buddha is the foremost; of all the liberators of the world, the sangha is the foremost." The wisdom and eloquence of Aryadeva brought Mahayana Buddhism to all of India.

Although Aryadeva had composed many works on Buddhism, only a few of these have survived. Among them, the most prominent is the *Treatise in Four Hundred Verses* (*Catuhsataka-sastra*). However, it was the determination of Aryadeva to oust the heretics that brought him to a violent death. In his last years, a successful repudiation of one heretic had led one of the his followers to take vengeance on Aryadeva. The killer ranted as he stabbed Aryadeva,"You have slashed my master with your words; how does it compare with my gutting you with this knife?"

Despite the wounds he sustained, Aryadeva remained calm. Without a trace of hatred or resentment, he took pity on the killer and asked him to escape. Before he passed away, Aryadeva wrote in his own blood the *Treatise in One Hundred Words*, his last revelation on the Dharma and final advice to his followers. To quote: "the true reality of all phenomena is that there is no one who is hurt and no one who hurts. Who is there to be a friend and who is there to be an enemy? Who is the offender and who is the victim? Duped by the poison of delusion, the false view of attachment arises to cause upheaval and generate unwholesome karma. He who sets off to hurt has not hurt me but rather himself through karmic retribution. All of you please deliberate! Take heed not to go after frenzy with impetuousness, or to offset grief with more sorrow!"

As successor to Nagarjuna, Aryadeva further advanced the Mahayana teaching of emptiness. In his willingness to sacrifice his life to attack deviant views and to foster concern rather than hatred for his killer, Aryadeva had lived out the true meaning of emptiness and selflessness. In India, his promotion of the study of emptiness had provided an impetus for the rapid progress of the Madhyamaka School.[55] In China, his teachings had rendered a positive impact on the development of the Chan School, and he was venerated as the second Patriarch of the The Middle Way School.

Aryadeva had weeded out the heretics with his sword of wisdom and bravery. In doing so, he widened the prospects for Mahayana Buddhism. His last breath was spent exhorting others to depart from deviant views and adhere to the truth. His rapport with Nagarjuna and the fact that he lost his life as a result of his dedication to his cause are a glorious page in Buddhist history. His admirable spirit will live on in the hearts of all Buddhists.

---

[55] The Madhyamaka School was founded on Nagarjuna's *Treatise on the Middle Way*, advocating the concept of emptiness. It unified the ideas of emptiness and skillful means, relative and ultimate truth, the mundane and supramundane world, and affliction and nirvana.

CHAPTER TWELVE

Asanga

The Founder of Consciousness Only

The "Consciousness Only" doctrine is known for its complex exegetical principles and terminology. It is said that followers of this school must be very patient to develop the clarity of mind necessary to fully appreciate its doctrine.

Since the early period of the Agamas, historical Buddhist thought gradually matured, culminating in the period of the Prajna and the Madhyamaka. The popular acceptance of the "Consciousness Only" doctrine that followed constituted a major leap forward in the history of Buddhist thought in that it became a major influence on the subsequent advancement in the study of anthropology. The founder of the "Consciousness Only" school is Asanga, the originator of this strand of Buddhist thought.

Asanga was born as a Brahman between 310 and 390 CE in Gandhara, Northern India, and was brought up under a strict Brahman education. In search for the truth about life, Asanga abandoned his inheritance to the esteemed position of Brahman Grand Master. Instead, he ordained under the Sarvastivadin School to practice the Hinayana way of contemplating emptiness. However, it was not until he met Maitreya of Ayodyha in Central India that Asanga realized the Mahayana view of emptiness. Maitreya instructed him on Mahayana teachings such as the *Commentary on the Stages of Yogacara Practitioners* (*Yogacara-bhumi-sastra*), the *Treatise on the Mahayana Adornment Sutra*, and *Treatise on the Different Stages of Yogacara Practitioners*. Soon afterwards, the Mahayana branch of "Consciousness Only" began to flourish and Asanga came to be hailed as one of the most outstanding sastra masters since Nagarjuna.

The "Consciousness Only" doctrine states that the pure seed of the supramundane world results from three things: learning about the Dharma; orienting oneself towards the habit of cultivation; and the actual practice of moral discipline, meditative concentration, wisdom and the Six Perfections. The consistent cultivation of merit and wisdom will gradually transform one's consciousness into wisdom,[56] and then one will attain nirvana and Buddhahood. Asanga's ideas were inspired by the Madhyamaka view of emptiness and are explanations of the Mahayana concepts of emptiness and compassion. In formulating a doctrine on the study of consciousness, Asanga pioneered a field of thought that was to become a hallmark in the Mahayana Buddhist history of India. He hence became the first to propagate the philosophy of "Consciousness Only" in India, and was also the founder of the Yogacara School of Mahayana Buddhism.

Although Asanga was the founder of the Mahayana Yogacara School, his younger brother Vasubandhu was initially a follower of Hinayana practice who announced that "Mahayana

---

[56] The Yogacara and Consciousness Only Schools believe that one can transform their eight consciousnesses (the five senses, the mind, the sense of self, and the *alaya* consciousness) from being defiled to being undefiled, and obtain the four kinds of wisdom (the wisdom of perfect conduct, the discriminating wisdom of profound insight, the wisdom of universal equality and the perfect mirror-like wisdom.)

teachings were not the Buddha's teachings." Although he launched vicious attacks on the Mahayana, Vasubandhu finally came to accept its teachings as a better way to attain the Buddha way under his brother's skillful guidance. In fact, Vasubandhu wanted to show remorse for his former slanderous attacks on Mahayana teachings by cutting off his own tongue. But Asanga's exhortation was that "such an act would not help to right the wrong he had done; repentance would only be effective if a pledge were made to henceforth spread the teachings of the Mahayana." Soon after this incident, Asanga passed away at the age of seventy-five. Vasubandhu followed his brother's vow to propagate Mahayana Buddhism by writing more sastras to expound its thoughts.

While Asanga was the founder of the Mahayana concept of "Consciousness Only," Vasubandhu was the one who consolidated this school of thought. Their concerted efforts opened a new era in Indian Buddhist history that was the highest development of Mahayana Buddhism since Nagarjuna and Aryadeva. Asanga's life-long dedication to the propagation of Mahayana Buddhism had not only contributed enormously to the Yogacara School, but also deeply influenced the study of Buddhism in China, Tibet and Japan. The two brothers were figures of great significance in Indian Buddhism, and the episode of Vasubandhu's conversion to the Mahayana has become legendary in Buddhist history.

Significant Works of Asanga:

> *Treatise on the Acclamation of the Noble Teachings*
>   *(Prakaranaryavaca-sastra)*
> *Explanation of the Treatise on Following the Middle Way*
> *Treatise on the Diamond Sutra (Vajracchedika-*
>   *prajnaparamitopadesa Sutra)*
> *Summary of Mahayana Doctrines*
> *Treatise on the Collection of Mahayana Abhidharma*
>   *(Mahayanabhidharma Samuccaya Vyakhya).*

CHAPTER THIRTEEN

Vasubandhu

The Master of a Thousand Treatises

There is a saying, "The Buddha enunciated the Dharma with one voice, but sentient beings understand it in many different ways." After the Buddha entered parinirvana, there soon developed what is known in Buddhist history as the Sectarian Period, from which emerged the branches of Hinayana and Mahayana Buddhism. However, no matter how diverse the schools might appear to be, "Dharma is originally of one taste — there is no other and no differentiation." Both the Hinayana and the Mahyana have their source in the Buddha's teachings, and the person most distinguished in assimilating the best of both to further expound on the Buddha's teachings was Vasubandhu.

Estimated to have been born between 320 and 400 CE, Vasubandhu was ordained under the Sarvastivadin School and aggressively launched attacks on the Mahayana through his commentaries. But after he was convinced by his brother to turn to Mahayana Buddhism, Vasubandhu dedicated himself wholeheartedly towards the dissemination of the "Consciousness Only" doctrine. Since then, the two brothers became central figures of the "Consciousness Only" School.

Coming from a Brahman family, Vasubandhu was precociously intelligent, and was particularly strong in the science of logic[57] and debate. After his ordaination, he studied the philosophy of the Sautrantika School with the intention to modifty and improve upon the doctrine of the Sarvastivadin School. He summarized their treatises in the *Summary of the Annotation of the Treatise on the Journey into Dharma (Abhidharma-kosa-sastra)*, a treatise of six hundred verses meant to challenge the *Annotation of the Treatise on the Journey into Dharma (Abhidharmahavibhasa-sastra)*, much to the distaste and envy of a famous heretical sastra master who retaliated by compelling the famous sastra master Samghabhadra of the Sarvastivadin School to produce the *Abhidharma-nyayanusasa* to rebuff Vasubandhu's literary onslaught. Had it not been for the forgiving and passive nature of Vasubandhu, this scathing exchange would have escalated into an open conflict. In the end, Samghabhadra reached an understanding with Vasubandhu, who actually renamed the *Abhidharma-nyayanusasa* the *Treatise on Following the Truth* to give it a wider circulation.

It is fitting for Vasubandhu to be honored as "Master of a Thousand Sastras." His treatises comprise five hundred compositions from his early Hinayana days as well as another five hundred treatises written on the Mahayana. The *Abhidharma-kosa-sastra* is considered the masterpiece of his Hinayana works. Rendered with great erudition and clarity, this sastra provides essential materials for gaining insight into Sectarian Buddhism and the basis upon which Mahayana thought was founded. Since then, the sastra has been honored as

[57] One of the five sciences (grammar and composition, arts and mathematics, medicine, logic, and philosophy) in India.

one of the important texts in Buddhism.

Since they were transmitted into China, many of his works became responsible for the development of the mainstream schools of Chinese Buddhism. For example, the Dasabhumika School[58] was founded on the the *Treatise on the Ten Stages Sutra*; the Pure Land School relied heavily on the *Treatise on the Pure Land Sastra* as a reference; the Shelun School[59] had its roots in the *Explanation on the Summary of Mahayana Doctrines*; the Abhidharma School[60] was established as a result of research into the *Abhidharma-kosa Sastra*; and the *Treatise on the Demonstration of Consciousness Only* as translated by Xuanzang became the scripture of the Consciousness Only School.[61]

It is common knowledge among Buddhist scholars that it takes at least three years of solid study to fully appreciate the thought expounded in the "Consciousness Only" doctrine and eight years to understand the *Abhidharma-kosa*. In other words, it takes at least ten years for scholars to comprehend the quantity and quality of the thought formulated by Vasubandhu. The period of Vasubandhu's contribution to the exposition of the Dharma coincided with the golden age of Indian Buddhism. Legend has it that when his teacher was being insulted by the heretics, Vasubandhu wrote the *Treatise of the Seventy Truths* to criticize the *Treatise of Sankhya* of the heretics. To show his approval and support for Vasubandhu's action, the king of Ayodhya awarded him a large sum of gold. With this award,

[58] This school advocated the dependent origination of the *tathagatagarbha*.
[59] This school advocated the doctrine of pure consciousness only, and the nine kinds of consciousness (the five senses, the mind, the sense of self, *alaya*, and *amala*), and taught that pure knowledge (*amala*) could be obtained by countering *alaya*.
[60] Based on the Hinayana Sarvastivadin School, it taught that all things arise due to causes and conditions, the absence of a self, and liberation from the three realms (the desire realm, the form realm, and the formless realm) through ending delusion.
[61] This school taught that all phenomena arise from consciousness. Xuanzang is regarded as the founder of this school.

Vasubandhu built three monasteries. The king took refuge under him while the prince took transmission of the precepts. One of the king's consorts chose to be ordained and became a disciple of Vasubandhu, and after the prince had ascended to the throne, Vasubandhu was invited by him and the queen mother to stay in Ayodhya to receive their offerings.

Due to the trust and respect that the two successive Gupta[62] rulers had in Vasubandhu during that time, Nalanda University, the most renowned Buddhist academy in India, was allowed to be expanded and reconstructed. During the time of its redevelopment, both Mahayana and Hinayana scholars flocked in to spread the Dharma. This surge of Buddhist intellectuals sparked off a revival of the Madhyamaka School, and the appearance of such brilliant figures as Silabhadra, Bhavaviveka, Simharasmi and Jnanaprabha returned to the glorious days of Nagarjuna and Aryadeva.

Written in the later years of his life, Vasubandhu's *Thirty Verses on Consciousness Only* was a work that astounded all scholars of "Consciousness Only" in India. Besides being the verses that were most widely read and studied, it became an indispensable reference work in the later study of "Consciousness Only."

Vasubandhu passed away at the age of eighty in Ayodhya. The Consciousness Only School founded by him and his brother Asanga was subsequently transmitted into China. The Consciousness Only School came to be known, together with the Madhyamaka School founded by Nagarjuna, as the two most important schools of Mahayana Buddhism in China.

---

[62] The Gupta Empire (280-550CE) unified southern and northern India and thrived between 320 and 470CE. It was the greatest patron of Buddhism since the end of the Mauryan Kingdom, and the most glorious period in the history of Indian culture.

Significant Works of Vasubandhu:

Summary of Mahayana Doctrines
*Twenty Verses on Consciousness Only (Vimsatika-
     vijnapti-matratasiddhi)*
*Thirty Verses on Consciousness Only (Trisika-vijnapti-
     matratasiddhi)*
Treatise on the Ten Stages Sutra
*Explanation of the Commentary on the Vyuharaja
     Sutra.*
Commentary on the Flower Ornament Sutra
Commentary on the Nirvana Sutra
Commentary on the Lotus Sutra
Commentary on the Prajna Sutra
Commentary on the Vimalakirti Sutra
Commentary on the Lion's Roar of Queen Srimala Sutra

CHAPTER FOURTEEN

Queen Srimala

One Who Undertook Ten Great Vows

Queen Srimala is an ideal Upasika (Buddhist female lay practitioner) and an exemplary devotee. The only daughter of King Prasenajit and Queen Mallika, Srimala was wife to King Oudh of Ayodhya. She became a Buddhist under the influence of her parents, who were both devout followers of the Buddha. However, not all members of her family were of the same mind. Out of hatred for the Sakya clan, her brother, Prince Virudhaka, flouted his military prowess by invading Kapilavatthu and decimating the Sakyans.

Before Srimala was born, King Prasenajit had been very worried about not having an heir. His earnest prayers for children were soon answered when the Queen gave birth to a girl. They named her Srimala as a reminder of the plentiful garlands and precious gifts offered by the people of Kosala at their daughter's birth. The name literally means that no treasure can match the outward beauty and inner wisdom of the princess.

Srimala had taken refuge in Buddhism, and deeply trusted and venerated the Buddha. Impressed by his wife's constant praise for the Buddha, the king of Ayodhya soon followed suit and took refuge as a Buddhist. Together, the couple began to

88

propagate the Buddha's teachings among their subjects. They were particularly dedicated to childhood education and organized regular classes for children over seven years of age that were held in the palace. In this respect, they might actually have been pioneers of the Sunday schools and cub-scout activities of modern times. Srimala was equally enthusiastic about improving the lives of women. She greatly emphasized the importance of "fetal education" for expectant mothers, and supported the belief that a woman's virtues are reflected in her role as a good mother and a good wife. She advocated that the priority in a woman's life goals should be to create a haven of happiness for her family.

Once, Srimala was asked by King Prasenajit to make a special trip back to Sravasti to hear the Buddha's teach the Dharma. During the assembly, the Buddha extolled Srimala's fervent faith in the Dharma and foretold that she would become a Buddha at the end of twenty thousand asamkheyakalpas (denoting a very long period of time) named Tathagata of Universal Light. This was a testimony to Queen Srimala's high level of attainment which was estimated to be equivalent to that of a Seventh or Eighth Stage Bodhisattva.[63]

Recorded in the the *Sutra of Mahayana Lion's Roar of Queen Srimala One-Vehicle Great and Profound Sutra of Skillful Means*[64] dispensed by the Buddha in the Jetavana Vihara of Sravasti are the Ten Great Vows of Queen Srimala, also known as the Ten Great Precepts or Ten Great Resolutions. They read as follows:

---

[63] Ten levels of faith, ten levels of dwelling, ten levels of practice, ten levels of dedication of merit, ten stages, equal enlightenment, and supreme enlightenment. The seventh stage is the stage of proceeding afar; the eighth stage is the attainment of calm.
[64] Translated by Gunavrddhi of the Southern Song Dynasty, it is one of the best representations of the *tathagatagarbha* doctrine in Mahayana Buddhism. It describes the Ten Great Resolutions and the Three Great Vows that Queen Srimala pledged to the Buddha.

Lord Buddha, from this day onwards until I realize bodhi, the intention to transgress any precepts that I have accepted to observe will definitely not arise in my mind.

Lord Buddha, from this day onwards until I realize bodhi, the thought of denigrating any venerable or elder will definitely not arise in my mind.

Lord Buddha, from this day onwards until I realize bodhi, the sense of hatred or resentment towards any sentient being will definitely not arise in my mind.

Lord Buddha, from this day onwards until I realize bodhi, the feeling of jealousy towards other people's happiness, beauty and fortune will definitely not arise in my mind.

Lord Buddha, from this day onwards until I realize bodhi, I will readily give all that I possess and all that I know to those in need, and I will definitely not harbor any selfish or miserly thoughts.

Lord Buddha, from this day onwards until I realize bodhi, I will not accumulate wealth for myself but will use all of it to relieve the suffering and poverty of sentient beings.

Lord Buddha, from this day onwards until I realize bodhi, I will not practice the Four Means of Embracing for my own benefit but will simply embrace all beings with a mind that is pure, unrelenting and fearless.

Lord Buddha, from this day onwards until I realize bodhi, I will certainly do my best to help those mired in solitude, sorrow, sickness and stress to be rid of their suffering before my mind will settle in peace.

Lord Buddha, from this day onwards until I realize bodhi, I will not falter in upholding righteousness and will adopt the most appropriate means to deal with people and matters that might cause harm to others.

Lord Buddha, from this day onwards until I realize bodhi, I vow to receive and to practice wholesome Dharma without reservation.

The contents of these Ten Great Vows are closely related to those of the *Three Collective Precepts of Purification (Tri-Vidhani Silani.)*[65] The first five are in essence the same as the *Collection of Rules on Discipline*, the sixth to the ninth correspond to the *Rules of Benefiting Sentient Beings*, and the tenth is equivalent to the precept vowing to fulfill all wholesome Dharmas. In addition to these ten vows, Queen Srimala also initiated three great vows. The first was to uphold the spirit of wholesome Dharma; the second was to disseminate wholesome Dharma throughout the world; and the third was to protect wholesome Dharma to ensure it would not degenerate.

In the Buddhist history of both India and China, the *Lion's Roar of Queen Srimala Sutra* is regarded as a very important sutra. It is considered by Buddhist scholars to be a major work on the doctrine of the *Dependent Origination of the Tathagatagarbha*.[66] The sutra's spirit is founded upon skillful means as expounded in the *Lotus Sutra* and the concepts of the pure mind and wondrous existence as declared in the *Flower*

---

[65] This refers to the three sets of Mahayana bodhisattva precepts: the precepts to eliminate wrongdoing and prevent unwholesomeness, the precepts to fulfill all wholesome Dharmas and attain Buddhahood, and the precepts to benefit all sentient beings.

[66] The Tathagatagarbha is the pure Dharma body of the Tathagata that is within all sentient beings, but is hidden by their afflictions. Though the *Tathagatagarbha* is hidden by the afflictions, it is not defiled by them, but remains permanently perfect and pure. All pure and impure phenomena are teachings that arise depending on the *Tathagatagarbha*. This is called the "Dependent Origination of the *Tathagatagarbha*."

Ornament Sutra.[67] It skillfully integrates the essence of these two sutras to develop the the study of the *Sutra on Understanding the Profound Doctrines* conception of the dependent origination of the alaya consciousness in the Consciousness Only School. The sutra also promotes the concept of the Tathagatagarbha being in affliction and features the discussion of the defiled world arising from the alaya consciousness.

The great virtue and merit of Queen Srimala was truly amazing. As a bodhisattva who practiced and propagated the teachings of the One Vehicle, it was doubtless that Queen Srimala would eventually attain Buddhahood.

---

[67] The *Lotus Sutra* and the *Flower Ornament Sutra* are early Mahayana sutras, while the *Lion's Roar of Queen Srimala* is from the middle period. *The Lotus Sutra* emphasizes having faith is the "one vehicle" of liberation. The *Flower Ornament Sutra* teaches that the mind, the universe, and the Buddha are the same, and emphasizes the practice of the fifty-two levels of a bodhisattva. The *Lion's Roar of Queen Srimala* teaches the doctrine of the Tathagatagarbha and the "one vehicle."

CHAPTER FIFTEEN

Vimalakirti

The Sutra and the Man

Of all the Buddhist writings, the *Vimalakirti Sutra*[68] is significant for its literary value. The central figure depicted in the sutra is an exceptional lay practitioner named Vimalakirti.

Vimalakirti is said to have planted virtuous seeds in previous lives and attained Buddhahood long ago as the Golden Grain Tathagata. It is believed that he manifested as a human and resided in the city of Vaisali, and was known to others as Upasaka Spotless Reputation or Undefiled. He was described as a lay practitioner who, "despite being clothed in white (i.e. of Brahman descent), strictly observed the pure precepts of a novice monk; although leading the home life, was not attached to the three realms; and behind the show of having a wife, was actually living in pure cultivation." With the outward appearance of a lay practitioner, Vimalakirti demonstrated incredible supernatural powers and spoke on the wondrous Dharma. He rebuked Hinayana practice as useless and fruitless, instructed bodhisattvas

[68] This sutra is a work of art presented as a dramatic and philosophical narrative between key Buddhist figures and a layman named Vimalakirti. The sutra was translated at least four times during the 150 years from Zhiqian of the Three Kindoms Period to Kumarajiva of the Eastern Jin Dynasty. It was not only a popular sutra at the time, but is now highly regarded both as a work of literature and as a Buddhist text and seen as highly influential in the development of Chinese thought.

94

on the ultimate practice of non-duality, and warned devotees of the importance of actively practicing the bodhisattva path to attain Buddhahood.

The Chinese translation of the *Vimalakirti Sutra* has deeply affected the studies of literature and philosophy[69] in China, and Vimalakirti the person has become an icon in the hearts of lay and monastic practitioners alike. Master Sengzhao, a very famous monk in China, was only ordained after having read the *Vimalakirti Sutra*, and Yinhao, of the Eastern Jin Dynasty, chanted the sutra as his daily practice. Confucian scholars and academics were most impressed by the *Vimalakirti Sutra*, and many of them aspired to write and live like the great Upasaka. The more famous of these included Xie Lingyun of the Southern Dynasty, Bai Juyi of the Tang Dynasty, Su Dongpo of the Song Dynasty, and Wang Wei of the Tang Dynasty, who actually adopted a pseudonym derived from the name Vimalakirti.

Vimalakirti advocated that bodhisattvas should not put an end to conditioned dharmas nor abide in unconditioned dharmas. Not ending conditioned dharma means to enter the cycle of birth and death without trepidation and receive glory and insult without a stir in the mind. Not abiding in unconditioned dharmas means, though one is aware of worldly suffering, one is not resentful of the cycle of birth and death but tirelessly guides others to the right path, despite having perceived the truth of non-self.

The *Vimalakirti Sutra* is described as being very critical of the Hinayana and extremely supportive of the Mahayana. In each of the sutra's fourteen chapters, light but revealing stories about bodhisattvas and arhats are told. The primary message of

---

[69] The profound and abstruse philosophy of the Vimalakirti Sutra was intensely loved by philosophers and metaphysicists.

the sutra is that there is "no fixed appearance in men and women, no fixed standard in the measurement of time, and no fixed scale in the concept of large and small." The thoughts of the deluded mind are diverse and changeable; hence everything worldly is subject to differentiation and relativity. It is only in the true and absolute mind that the Pure Land can be realized, and such a state of being is encompassed in compassion and in the spirit of benefiting others. In other words, the Pure Land is epitomized in the Mahayana dictum of "performing a worldly career with a supramundane mind."

The *Vimalakirti Sutra* encourages the realization of the Bodhisattva Pure Land, which is the "Pure Land of Mind Only." This is "a pure land evoked entirely by the purity of mind" and it is therefore possible to attain in this world. In blending the Buddha's teachings with everyday life, Vimalakirti applied the Dharma in daily activities and created a pure land in this world. The following are deemed conducive to attaining the Pure Land state in this world for the practitioner:

1. Regard prajna wisdom as your kindly mother.
2. Regard wholesome skillfulness as your strict father.
3. Regard meditative joy and Dharma joy as your spouse.
4. Regard gentleness and compassion as your daughter.
5. Regard honesty and kindness as your son.
6. Regard all proper practices as your knowledge.
7. Regard the Six Perfections and their ten thousand practices as your Dharma friends.
8. Regard the pure water that cleanses the mind as what quenches your thirtst.
9. Regard the wondrous taste of liberation as your lecture hall.
10. Regard the dignified and adorned image as your body.

11. Regard cultivation with contrition as your clothing.
12. Regard the health of body and mind as your garland.
13. Regard ultimate tranquility[70] as your family.
14. Regard upholding the Buddha's intentions as your court and quarters.
15. Regard the Eight Methods of Attaining Liberation[71] as your bath.
16. Regard the Four Levels of Meditative Concentration[72] as your bedframe.
17. Regard the Five Supernatural Powers[73] as your elephants and horses.
18. Regard the Mahayana resolve as your means of transport.
19. Regard the single-mindedness to attain the Way as your travels.
20. Regard the general public as your teachers.
21. Regard afflictions as your followers.
22. Regard the Four Means of Embracing as your entertainers.
23. Regard the gathas and verses on Dharma as your music.
24. Regard the practice of meditation and Pure Land as your amusement.
25. Regard the Seven Properties of Virtue[74] as your treasure.
26. Regard the education of the next generation as your return on capital.

---

[70] All phenomena are ultimately unattainable due to their dependent nature. Tranquility comes from understanding the true nature of the emptiness of all phenomena, and thus breaking all attachments.
[71] Breaking through the attachments to forms and desires with the eight kinds of meditative concentraction.
[72] These four levels of meditative concentration eradicate illusion and cultivate virtue.
[73] The power to be anywhere and do anything at will, the power to see the suffering and happiness of all sentient beings, the power to hear any sound, the power to read minds, and the power to know all the past lives of oneself and others.
[74] The seven ways of attaining the Way: faith, precepts, shame, conscience, obedient hearing, giving, and wisdom arising from meditation.

27. Regard the transference of merit to all as your profit.
28. Regard the general resolution to attain the Way as your career.
29. Regard the unfaltering mind as your sanctuary.
30. Regard the extensive contact with wholesome Dharma as your voice of awakening.

It is hoped that everyone will be as witty and cheerful as Vimalakirti. To realize the pure land in this world, we should emulate his practice as summarized in the following gatha:

With courtesy, respect and kind words,
Come happiness, contentment and optimism.
Reason, peace and harmony will bring bountiful freedom,
And security can be celebrated as a result of compassion
And the capacity to accommodate others.

CHAPTER SIXTEEN

Young Bodhisattvas

Young people are at the heart of the Buddhist religion. While images of Buddhas and bodhisattvas all bear expressions of compassion and tranquility to represent peace and harmony, they are seldom seen to have beards or wrinkles. This is a clear symbol of the youth, purity, innocence, and compassion of the bodhisattva.

In Buddhism, the young are seen to be the embodiment of wisdom, intelligence, genuine zest and drive. The following are several young boys and girls depicted in the sutras to illustrate young bodhisattvas:

Sudhana

Of all the outstanding youths in the sutras, the one most well known is Sudhana. His image is usually found with Nagakanya the Dragon Maiden flanking the image of Avalokitesvara Bodhisattva in the shrines of most monasteries and temples. Born the son of an Elder, Sudhana was bright, veracious and full of vitality. It is recorded that on the day of his birth, his household was inundated with riches and valuables; hence he was named Sudhana, which means "wholesome wealth." On the recommendation of Manjusri Bodhisattva, Sudhana traveled to the South and visited fifty-three spiritual advisors[75] to seek their advice on cultivation. Such an exercise is considered helpful in training to subdue one's arrogance and cultivate humility, to disassociate with bad company, to gather good conditions for cultivation and to model oneself after the virtuous and accomplished. On Sudhana's epic journey he met with many bhiksus, bhiksunis, upasakas, and upasikas, as well as physicians, oarsmen, kings and king's consorts, until he finally received instructions on the practice of the Great Vows from Samanthabhadra Bodhisattva. The story of Sudhana lucidly indicates that it is most effective for young people to learn Buddhist teachings and put them into practice.

Yasa

Yasa,[76] from Kasi, was the first young man whom the Buddha encountered soon after his enlightenment. Yasa told the Buddha he was fed up with his lavish lifestyle and wanted to abandon his desires and pleasures for a life of purity. On hearing this, the Buddha exclaimed in delight, "Yasa, you certainly have good roots to want to abandon those things that are the source of afflictions and defilement. I can help you fulfill your wish!" The Buddha then taught the Dharma to Yasa, who was so moved that he implored the Buddha to ordain him. The Buddha told Yasa that he should first obtain permission from his parents. Yasa's father, an Elder, was anxiously looking for his son when he met the Buddha, who explained to him the unbecoming

---

[75] See the *Flower Ornament Sutra*. Samantabhadra Budhisattva was the last of the fifty-three that Sudhana visited and sought advice from. Sudhana attained Buddhahood after he had accomplished the Ten Great Vows of Samantabhadra Bodhisattva.

[76] Yasa was the sixth disciple of the Buddha. Later his lay parents and wife also took refuge in the Triple Gem and became the first upasaka and upasikas.

effects caused by ignorance of the truth, and the benefits of practicing generosity and upholding the precepts. The Elder was instantly awakened to the misery that accompanies worldly existence and willingly gave his consent for Yasa to become the Buddha's follower. Since Yasa was ordained, many more young men followed in his footsteps and joined the sangha.

Rahula

Before the Buddha renounced his life as a prince, he was married to Yasodhara, who gave birth to their only son, Rahula. Rahula was ordained at a very tender age and became the first child in the sangha to practice under the tutelage of Sariputra and abide by a set of regulations specially devised for novice monks.

Although the young Rahula was not accustomed to the sangha's way of life, he was very obedient and respectfully submitted to the instructions of Sariputra and the Buddha. Besides learning to practice the Buddha's teachings, Rahula had to do daily chores in the community and offer his services to help lay devotees. When bullied by older monks, Rahula would patiently endure their pranks. Once, Rahula had nowhere to stay but the outhouse because his room was taken. Heavy rain brought a snake into the outhouse, and everyone else was frightened and worried for him. To their surprise, Rahula remained calm and composed. There were other times when Rahula would play tricks on visitors to the monastery. On being reprimanded by the Buddha for this mischief, he would immediately change his ways for the better. Due to his patience, willingness to learn and arduous practice, Rahula soon attained arhatship. He was the youngest of the Buddha's Ten Great Disciples to have reached such an attainment.

There are of course many other young men mentioned in the sutras who are exemplary in their own ways, but Rahula's qualities of tolerance and steadfastness in practice well deserve praise and emulation.

Sumati

Sumati is described in the the *Sutra of Great Treasures* as a young girl with profound wisdom and resolute determination. She was the daughter of a dignitary from Rajagriha in Magadha who often attended the Buddha's Dharma assemblies at Vulture Peak even as early as when she was only eight years old.

Sumati was pretty, gentle and demure. Once, while the Buddha was teaching the Dharma, she calmly walked up to the Buddha. Having shown her respect by prostrating herself three times to pay homage to the Buddha, she posed ten questions to the Buddha for his advice. All those present at the assembly were astonished to see such a young girl raise the following questions:

- How can we acquire a decent and wholesome body?
- How can we acquire great wealth and high prestige?
- How can we prevent poor health, death, and disharmony in the family?
- How can we be seated upon a large jeweled lotus like the Buddha?
- How can we be able to travel to the various Buddha lands to pay homage to all Buddhas?
- How can we avoid having enemies and rivals?
- How should we speak to induce faith in others?
- How should we practice to eliminate obstacles and hindrances?
- How can we be rid of the afflictions and obstructions of Mara?

- How can we have the chance to see the Buddha and listen to the Dharma?

Even Manjusri Bodhisattva commended Sumati on her courage and merit.

Bhadda Kapilani

Bhadda Kapilani was a beautiful and virtuous girl who was betrothed to the young and eligible Mahakasyapa. After much deliberation, however, both of them agreed to maintain their pure practice and went their separate ways to pursue spiritual cultivation. Bhadda Kapilani followed a heretic at first, but soon turned to the Buddha for proper guidance and was ordained and became his follower. While she went on her alms round as a bhiksuni, Bhadda Kapilani was often teased by the public for her extraordinary beauty. This made her realize that physical beauty could sometimes be a nuisance. However, her simple nature and devotion helped her concentrate on her practice, and she soon attained arhatship.

The Celestial Maiden Who Rained Flowers

It is recorded in the *Vimalakirti Sutra* that when Upasaka Vimalakirti became ill, he was paid a visit by the great arhats and bodhisattvas. Among the attendants busying themselves in the room was a young and beautiful maiden. Sariputra was ill at ease with her presence because he considered it improper for men and women to mix in a place of Buddhist practice. A feeling of contempt for the girl arose in his mind.

The Celestial Maiden read the mind of Sariputra and rained flowers from the heavens onto the crowd. Blossoms that came down on the great bodhisattvas instantly fell to the ground, but those that landed on Sariputra and the great arhats clung to their bodies. As Sariputra was struggling to remove the flowers from his robe, the Celestial Maiden said to him, "Venerable Sariputra, why are you so eager to get rid of the flowers?" Holding back his restlessness, Sariputra replied, "I have to remove them because it is not in accord with the Dharma to have flowers on my body!" Still smiling, the Celestial Maiden said, "Venerable one! You cannot say that this floral presence is not in accord with the Dharma. Flowers have no sense of differentiation; it is only in the Venerable's own mind that differentiation abounds! It is actually in discord with the Dharma for those who have renounced to follow the Buddha to breed differentiation in their minds!" The great arhat was dumbfounded by the maiden's words.

There are many other young maidens of great wisdom and virtue recorded in the sutras, the most well known being the Dragon Girl[77] from the *Lotus Sutra*, who attained Buddhahood at the age of eight. Her story shows that wisdom in young girls can be the same as that of the great sages and bodhisattvas. In Buddhism all beings possess the primordial nature of pure wisdom. Hence, the potential for attainment is basically equal between men and women, young and old.

---

[77] Daughter of the Naga king Sagara. She often listened to the Buddha's teachings and instantly attained Buddhahood at the age of eight.

Chapter Seventeen

The Characteristics of a
Modern Bodhisattva

The term bodhisattva is commonly used today to denote people with the vow and intent to benefit the general public. As the sutras say, "To become accomplished in Buddhist practice, one should first be of service to the public, like horses and steers." This shows the determination and compassion that is necessary for a bodhisattva. On the path to attaining Buddhahood, it is initially necessary to nurture these bodhisattva qualities by cherishing affinities with people.

Anyone who resolves to benefit others can be called a bodhisattva, and historically the bodhisattva has always been a symbol of wisdom and compassion, resolve and practice. In adapting to the modern world, the bodhisattvas of today should manifest the following characteristics.

They need to have an accommodating and cheerful personality that epitomizes compassion and loving kindness

The fact that the Buddha had tirelessly propagated the Dharma throughout the Ganges region of India for forty-nine years demonstrates his dedication to benefiting others. Maitreya Bodhisattva, who led a carefree and contented life, is a typical example of a tolerant and happy character. All of the Buddha's Ten Great Disciples took it as their mission to spread the way of true happiness to the world, and they carried with them a capacity to accommodate critics from other faiths. It was out of true compassion that Maudgalyayana forgave the heretics who ambushed him, and Sariputra empathized with those who attempted to defame him. A bodhisattva would never give up on any sentient being, be they indomitable or unrepentant. By inspiring others with faith and happiness, a bodhisattva helps to raise the hopes of all.

They need to protect the Dharma and safeguard Buddhist teachings without trepidation

During their long period of cultivation, bodhisattvas must confront many difficulties with patience before they can move forward. Enduring adverse circumstances, especially slander and ridicule, calls for unlimited courage. One can recall the martyrdom of Aryadeva in defending the right Dharma or the great vow of Ksitigarbha Bodhisattva to liberate all beings from hell. These are prominent examples of selfless courage. Although bodhisattvas usually appear calm and sedate, they sometimes show outrage to express disapproval or condemnation. These are but skillful means to deal with individuals of different roots.

It is said that, "The propagation of the Dharma is primarily the duty of the sangha." In the continuous transmission of Buddhism, monastic bodhisattvas should always tell themselves that "Buddhism relies on me." Dissemination of the right Dharma and the protection of Buddhism are part of a bodhisattva practice, without which Buddhism would never have survived the several fierce persecutions it suffered in the history of

China.[78] It is only through the concerted efforts of innumerable bodhisattvas that the Dharma wheel has kept turning, and the bodhisattva spirit of fearlessness and sacrifice has enabled Buddhism to prevail.

They need to practice their faith along the principles of the Mahayana doctrine

The practice of bodhisattvas requires placing equal emphasis on the cultivation of merit and wisdom. The *Sutra on the Collection of the Six Perfections states*, "Practicing what they preach, bodhisattvas embrace all sentient beings, like the light of the sun and the moon nurturing all things." Besides amassing meritorious virtue through deeds of compassion and courage, it is crucial for bodhisattvas to have boundless faith and resolve before they can realize the Mahayana ideal of helping sentient beings find liberation.

As stated in the *Chapter on Ascetic Practices in the Flower Ornament Sutra*, "To practice the Mahayana faith is to eliminate all unwholesomeness, to embrace all wholesomeness and live by the Dharma without walls in the mind." By fully understanding the teachings and precepts, and having deportment that inspires respect, humility, and contrition, bodhisattvas acquire insight into the equality of all sentient beings. It is only with such an understanding that greed, anger and delusion can be totally eradicated.

It was out of an aspiration to accomplish the Mahayana ideal of practicing giving that Elder Sudatta[79] was so generous

---

[78] There were fierce persecutions of Buddhism in the Northern Wei, Northern Zhou, Tang, Latter Zhou, Ming, and Qing Dynasties, and even during the Culture Revolution.

[79] An elder who lived at Sravasti in Central India, Sudatta was wealthy and kind and often donated food and clothing to orphans and old people. Hence, he was also called Anathapindika (the one who takes care of widows and orphans.) He presented the Buddha with the Jetavana Vihara after taking refuge in him.

with his offerings and Sariputra so ready to donate his own eyes. Similarly, the bhiksu who would not transgress the precepts even though he had already taken on the body of a goose,[80] and Ksantyrsi, who silently suffered insult and bred no hatred toward Kaliraja for mutilating him, and Prince Sudana, who was always generous without reservation,[81] are examples of bodhisattvas with a truly Mahayana spirit.

They need to apply skillful means to liberate sentient beings

The actions of bodhisattvas should involve methods that pertain to both the worldly and the supramundane. Using skillful means to deliver sentient beings begins with creating affinities with others. It is only then that the skillful means implied in the Four Means of Embracing (Catuh-samgraha-vastu) and the Four Skillful Means to teach the Dharma of the four Siddantanta[82] can be applied. The Five Great Bodhisattvas are known to have their own special ways to inspire sentient beings. Avalokitesvara uses his compassion, Manjusri uses his wisdom, Ksitigarbha uses his great vows, Samantabhadra uses his practices, and Maitreya uses his benevolence. The great monastics of the past also effectively liberated sentient beings by using their individual skills.

Four eminent monks of the twentieth century demonstrated their own skillful means. Master Xuyun inspired faith in people through his deep meditative concentration; Master Yinguang

---

[80] See the *Sutralamkara Sastra.*

[81] The prince was a previous incarnation of the Buddha, who was generous and charitable and often donated food, clothing, precious jewels, horse carriages, houses, and farmland—anything that people needed. He even gave his two sons to a Brahman.

[82] *Siddantanta* means "accomplished people," "perfected masters," or "doctrine." There are four such categories: analyzing the causes and conditions of the world, teaching according to the individual capacities of sentient beings, diagnosing the mental afflictions of sentient beings, and the supreme truth.

propagated Buddhist teachings through letters written to his followers and sutra publication; Master Hongyi spread the Dharma through his art and calligraphy; and Master Taixu contributed to the revitalization of Buddhism by applying his wisdom to reform the sangha.

The sutras say, "Compassion is the mother and skillful means the father." It is through compassion and skillful means that the Buddhas of the three time periods attain Supreme Enlightenment.

In fact, the characteristics of a modern bodhisattva are summarized in the Buddha's Light membership gatha:

> *May compassion, loving kindness, joy and equanimity*
> *pervade the universe;*
> *May all beings benefit from our blessings and friendship;*
> *May our ethical practice of Chan and Pure land help us*
> *achieve universal tolerance;*
> *May we undertake the great Mahayana vows in humility*
> *and gratitude.*

CHAPTER EIGHTEEN

The Attributes of a
Bodhisattva

The skillfullness and virtues of the bodhisattva has several different interpretations and sets of terminology in the sutras. For example, the *Flower Ornament Sutra* refers to bodhisattvas as "the Instructors," "the Great Ones," "the Empowered Ones," and "the Unsurpassed Ones." In the *Sutra of Bodhisattva Stages*, they are known as "Sons of the Buddha," "Great Masters," "Great Saints," "Great Names," "Great Virtues," and "the Greatly at Ease." The *Treatise on the Stages of Yogacara Practitioners* describes bodhisattvas as those who "can subdue all," "are brave and stalwart," "have pity and sympathy" and "are Dharma Masters." More precisely, the *Commentary on the Mind Seal of the Diamond Sutra* depicts the following seven aspects of the bodhisattva:

Endowment of Great Roots

Due to variations of their potential to hear, see, and think, sentient beings differ in their ability to understand the truth. As the "King of All Healers," the Buddha applied skillful means to cater to the needs of different people, with the ultimate aim of enlightening them to the truth and instilling in them the resolve to cultivate to be liberated from suffering.

It is through understanding the Four Noble Truths that sravakas attain the four holy fruits, while pratyekabuddhas are enlightened through their direct understanding of the Twelve Links of Dependent Origination. Bodhisattvas are motivated to initiate their great vows and perform their great deeds because they are rooted in great compassion and wisdom, and thus they can attain Supreme Enlightenment without retrogression.

Possession of Great Wisdom

The wisdom of bodhisattvas is the wisdom found in the Diamond Sutra: equanimity without differentiation. It is because of the presence of such wisdom that the mind is able to accommodate the boundless and regard all sentient beings as oneself, as stated in the *Lankavatara Sutra*. It is only with this mind that the oneness and coexistence[83] of all sentient beings is truly understood and all-embracing compassion is generated. It is stated in the *Lion's Roar of Queen Srimala Sutra* that "for the sake of all beings," bodhisattvas "speak the Dharma without the slightest feeling of boredom or displeasure."

The great wisdom of bodhisattvas transcends the trivialities of ordinary intellect, and can sever the defilements produced by mundane perceptions and illusory discernment. Such great wisdom gives rise to samadhi[84] concentration and, despite being detached from birth and death as well as nirvana, it can be utilized in unlimited ways. Avalokitesvara is the best example of this skillful means of teaching the Dharma.

---

[83] Here "oneness and coexistence" refers to equality and tolerance. Though there are many different countries, peoples, and regions in the world, we all rely on the same earth to exist. We can live in harmony if we realize this interdependence.

[84] Samadhi is clearly understanding that all phenomena are illusory and impermanent. Bodhisattvas abide in samadhi to realize these truths as well as to liberate all sentient beings. Thus they are not attached to either liberating sentient beings or abiding in nirvana.

Faith and conviction in the Great Dharma

Having thoroughly understood the true meaning of the doctrines of Dependent Origination and the Middle Way, bodhisattvas see no contradiction between emptiness and existence, and can thus fulfill their supramundane thoughts through worldly deeds. Bodhisattvas are fully aware that, though their actions are motivated by compassion, the success of their endeavors to benefit others is dependent on skillful means. They understand that "mind, Buddha and all beings are equal and undifferentiated," hence they follow the actions of Sadaparibhuta Bodhisattva and would never slight any sentient being. As they are no longer attached to the notions of self, others, sentient beings or longevity, they can give with genuine generosity and liberate sentient beings with the purest of intentions.

Perception of the Great Truth

Bodhisattvas perceive prajna wisdom as the mother of all Buddhas, and the reality of phenomenal existence as dependent upon the arising and ceasing of causes and conditions. They acknowledge the Three Dharma Seals as the universal truth, and that the four elements and five aggregates are the basis of life. They are fully aware that the principle that underlies existence is that of interdependence, and that practice in accordance with the thirty-seven practices to enlightenment is conducive to the enhancement of merit and wisdom. They understand that the way to attain Buddhahood is to learn from the Buddhas and liberate sentient beings. Bodhisattvas recognize that the Dharma body and suchness are the origin of life, which is without birth and death. Thus, through understanding the law of dependent origination, bodhisattvas have no aversion towards or delusions about birth and death.

Cultivation of magnanimous acts

The great acts of bodhisattvas consist of enduring the unbearable. Through many kalpas (three great asamkheyakalpas) of cultivation within the six realms of existence, the Buddha never missed an opportunity to perform a compassionate act or faltered for a moment in his original vows. As the lion king, he sacrificed his life to satisfy the craving of the hungry vulture. As a rabbit king, he set his own body on fire as an offering in order to hear the Dharma. As a golden deer, he bravely rescued the lives of his herd. As the King of Tranquility, he extracted his own blood everyday to treat the sick. As the Dragon King, he bred no hatred upon being skinned. Once as a ruler, he stabbed himself just to hear the revelations of half a gatha on the Dharma. As the king of the hares, he jumped into a snare so that his fellow hares could be released.[85]

Endurance of an extremely long period of cultivation

The length of time required for cultivation of the bodhisattva path is prescribed to be three great asamkheyakalpas. This is a very long period of time during which the fifty-one levels of attainment are accomplished. In the first great asamkheyakalpa, the practitioner mainly nurtures faith, cultivating the ten stages of faith, and then emptiness is realized. By the second asamkheyakalpa, practitioners have become saints or sages, and cultivate up to the seventh level of ground where the "state of formlessness" is realized. As practitioners enter the third asamkheyakalpa, they will attain the eighth level of ground. In this state there is no attachment to form or attainment, realization or enlightenment. They will

---

[85] These stories come from the *Jataka Tales*: stories of the Buddha's past lives in which he practices the bodhisattva path.

attain patience regarding the non-arising of dharmas, where the afflictions of the three realms are totally eradicated and the penultimate level to Buddhahood is attained.

Bodhisattvas are said to have good roots and great resolve. Throughout the long period of cultivation, they would have accumulated limitless merit and wisdom, and cultivated a dignified appearance. During this same period, they would have remained among sentient beings to liberate them with complete devotion.

Attainment of the Ultimate Fruit

"The ultimate fruit" refers to anuttara-samyak-sambodhi, Supreme Enlightenment. This is the perfect state that is free of defilement, hindrances, desires, resentment or delusion, as well as all dualistic concepts. Yet, as clearly indicated in the the the *Sutra on Understanding the Profound Doctrines*, bodhisattvas who have realized nirvana are motivated by their compassionate vows to manifest in the phenomenal world and be subject to the law of cause and effect. They exist throughout many lands in millions of manifestations to benefit sentient beings by proclaiming the right Dharma and performing good deeds.

Boundless compassion is inherent to Supreme Enlightenment, where there is no differentiation between birth and death or great and small. This state is described in the *Treatise on the Four Noble Truths* as "complete and perfect, pure, supreme suchness, free from worries, limitations, obstacles and desires." The progression from being a bodhisattva to attaining Buddhahood is both ineffable and incredible. As stated in the *Flower Ornament Sutra*, "To know the Buddha state, the mind needs to be as pure as the vastness of space." The Buddha taught that "to see the Law of Dependent Origination is to see the Buddha."

116

From the beginning of the bodhisattva path to the attainment of Buddhahood, practitioners acquire the great root of compassion and the great wisdom that grants them insight into emptiness. They gain faith and conviction in the Dharma of the Six Perfections and the Four Means of Embracing. They come to understand the ultimate truth that there is nothing to be attained or realized, yet they still undertake magnanimous acts to benefit others in the world of duality and relative notions. They become fearless to endure the long period of cultivation needed to realize the ten powers,[86] the four grounds of fearlessness,[87] and the eighteen unique merits[88] for the complete and perfect attainment of Buddhahood.

---

[86] The power of deep mind, power of the enhanced deep mind, power of skillful means, power of wisdom, power of vows, power of practice, power of vehicle, power of transformation, power of bodhi, power of turning the Dharma wheel. The *Surangama Samadhi Sutra*, and chapter 25 of the *Great Treatise on the Perfection of Wisdom* list several variations of the ten powers.

[87] Fearlessness of expounding the Dharma from what has been heard, fearlessness in expounding the Dharma appropriate to the capacities of sentient beings, fearlessness in countering an attack on the Buddhist teachings and removing doubt, and fearlessness in responding to questions; as stated in Chapter 5 of the *Great Treatise on the Perfection of Wisdom* and chapter 11 of the *Explanation of the Mahayana*.

[88] The eighteen unique merits of Buddhahood are found in Chapter 4 of the *Precious Rain Sutra*: (1) practicing generosity, not following other's teachings; (2) upholding precepts, not following other's teachings; (3) practicing patience, not following other's teachings; (4) maintaining diligence, not following other's teachings; (5) practicing silent contemplation, not following other's teachings; (6) cultivating prajna, not following other's teachings; (7) practicing in the collection of matters and including all sentient beings; (8) the ability to understand the dedication of merit; (9) using skillful means, guiding all sentient beings to practice, and being able to appear in the most supreme vehicle and attain liberation; (10) not retreating from the Mahayana; (11) the capability to appear in life, death, and nirvana and attain peace and joy, skillful language, and the ability to follow mundane customs; (12) being guided by wisdom and turning away from all wrongdoing; (13) possessing the ten wholesome actions; (14) including all sentient beings and not turning away from them, bearing all their suffering; (15) being able to display everything the world loves and enjoys; (16) not abandoning wisdom even when abiding in the suffering of ordinary people and sravakas; (17) Accepting the seat of the Dharma king and empowering it with silk and water; (18) being not far from the Buddha's wholesome Dharma and appearing at a sincere request.

CHAPTER NINETEEN

The Completion of the
Bodhisattva Path

To quote from the *Parable Chapter* of the *Lotus Sutra*, "Like an inferno that is filled with horror and suffering, the three realms offer no peace of mind."[89] It said in the *Worldly Views Chapter* of the *Dhammapada Sutra* that, "As death is inevitable in worldly existence, there can be no security in the three realms. There may indeed be happiness in celestial existence, but happiness ends when merits are exhausted."

Can sentient beings ever find peace of mind in the constant flow of afflictions that come with the cycle of birth and death? Wealth belongs to the five families[90] and cannot be accumulated forever. Our loved ones must part with us one day. Life is inundated with the eight distresses of rebirth within the six realms of existence.[91] What can we ultimately rely on to ensure that life is lived out wholesomely and to the fullest? The answer lies in aspiring for bodhi, or the initiation of the bodhi mind. It is

[89] One cannot find true peace in the desire realm, the form realm, or the formless realm.
[90] Mundane wealth belongs to the "five families:" kings, thieves, fire, water, and wayward sons. Wealth cannot belong to an individual, and thus there is no reason to demand it.
[91] birth, aging, sickness and death; the suffering of affliction, sorrow and grief; the suffering from association with the unloved; the suffering of separation from the loved; the suffering of unfulfilled desire.

118

through this vow to practice the bodhisattva path with the goal
of enlightenment and liberation both for oneself and others that
life can be made truly wholesome and meaningful.

Complete and perfect attainment of the bodhisattva path
requires being pure in body, speech, and mind. This necessitates
turning away from the five sensual desires,[92] subduing the four
obstacles of mara,[93] and being liberated from the fetters of
ignorance. Only then can the body and mind be truly at ease. At
the time of the Buddha, Uppalavanna[94] freed herself from the
delusion of love and became the bhiksuni foremost in the
supernatural power of traveling everywhere. Prince Bhadrika[95]
realized true happiness only after his ordination because he no
longer feared assassination. The knowledge Mahakasyapa[96] found
upon hearing the Dharma brought him great relief and he became
a leading figure among the sagely disciples of the Buddha. Having
reformed his false speech, Rahula[97] managed to purify his words
and thoughts and master the esoteric practices, becoming an
example for other young followers. At the exhortation of the
Buddha, Angulimala,[98] the mass murderer, was able to transform

[92] The desires of wealth, forms, food, fame, and sleep.
[93] The *mara* of the five aggregates, the *mara* of affliction, the *mara* of death, and the
celestial *mara* who is the king of the sixth heaven in the desire realm. This final *mara*
tries to prevent sentient beings from doing good.
[94] Among the Buddha's female disciples she is honored as the foremost in supernatural
powers.
[95] Said to be a son of king Amrtodana. He was taught by the Buddha at the Deer Park and
became one of the first five disciples of the Buddha,
[96] One of the Buddha's ten great disciples, foremost in asceticism. He became the leader
of the sangha after the Buddha's parinirvana, and convened the First Council.
[97] One of the Buddha's ten great disciples, formerly the Buddha's lay son. When he was a
novice monk there were many occasions when his actions were not in accordance with
the Dharma, and he was scolded by the Buddha. As a result he strictly upheld the
precepts, diligently practiced the Way, and became an arhat. He was honored as the
foremost in subtly observing the precepts.
[98] Meaning finger topknot, or all mundane appearances. Angulimala was depicted in the
sutras as a ruthless killer who is redeemed by converting to Buddhism; his story is seen
as an example of the redemptive power of the Buddha's teachings and the universal
human potential for spiritual progress.

the boiling hatred within him and become a model of patience and passivity. These examples show that to attain the bodhisattva path is to eradicate greed, anger, ignorance and delusion within us, and to nurture moral discipline, meditative concentration and prajna wisdom in their place.

Although the road of cultivation may be long and difficult, attaining the bodhisattva path is by no means impossible. It has been said that "attainment of being truly human implies the attainment of Buddhahood." This means that besides being the key to living a full and meaningful life, wholesome human conduct that incorporates high moral standards and the practice of compassion and loving kindness is a vital aspect of physical and mental purification. In this regard, the Five Great Bodhisattvas mentioned earlier provide the best examples for us to emulate. Those who have initiated bodhicitta should walk in their footsteps, earnestly protect the Triple Gem, propagate the right Dharma, and diligently cultivate wisdom to benefit all beings. To fully accomplish the bodhisattva path one must completely remove all defilements and generate the determination to liberate all sentient beings without discrimination. Practitioners should never forget their initial vow as stated in the *Flower Ornament Sutra*, and be a welcome friend as stated in the *Vimalakirti Sutra*; nor should they cling to past grievances as stated in the *Sutra of the Eight Realizations of Great Beings*. They should accept changes as they arise while remaining mindful of the unchanging and equal, primordial nature of all dharmas (phenomena), as stated in the *Treatise on the Awakening of Faith in Mahayana*. They should try to foster good affinities with all those who come their way so that others may also benefit from wholesome Dharma.

Bodhisattvas recall that the Buddha attained enlightenment only after he defeated Mara, the manifestation of the demons within. Those who vow to cultivate the Buddha way, should embrace the Six Perfections, practice the Four Means of Embracing and the Four Universal Vows. If they abide with right wisdom and practice the bodhisattva path they can transform the sea of suffering into peaceful bliss and tranquility in this present life.

Attainment of the Bodhisattva Path in the Family

Buddhism is a human-based religion, and in addition to skillfully teaching wise and practical methods for individual purification, the Buddha also helped his followers make their families more stable. For example, by liberating Sujata, daughter-in-law of Sudatta, the Buddha taught her to change her arrogant ways, thus preventing the imminent collapse of her marriage. Similarly, as a result of the Buddha's instructions to the young Susambhava he came to acknowledge the importance of filial duties and mutual respect in the family, thus saving him from falling into disgrace.

Do not be misled into the belief that husbands and wives are bound to have grudges against each other, that children are a liability, or that the family is a prison. Instead, the family should be seen as a Pure Land of support and respect, joy and harmony. For this to be possible, members of a family must adopt the right attitude. They must always be ready to share their views, see the best in their family members, respect one another, be there in times of trouble, and be a welcome friend to all beings. It is not difficult for Buddhist practitioners who have a good relationship with their families to see their entire family liberated.

Attainment of the Bodhisattva Path in Society

Our modern society is faced with many problems, including the threat of war, financial crises, ethnic conflicts, ecological disasters, welfare for the handicapped, an aging population, crime, unemployment, unequal distribution of wealth, domestic abuse and violence, as well as many other problems. To secure peace and stability in society, Buddhism advocates aspiring for unity. In order to truly manifest compassion and for harmony to prevail in this society we must respect human rights, value the right to live, develop tolerance and respect, accept our differences, and be aware of our common goals.

The Buddhist vision of an ideal society is one in which people live in a magnificent and open environment, where ecology can survive in its clean and orderly nature. Socially, people should interact with a spirit of kindness, amity, mutual encouragement and support. Daily necessities like food should be bountiful so that we can live a life in security and contentment. Economic activities should involve real productivity with a view to achieving an egalitarian state.

Attainment of the Bodhisattva Path in the Dharma Realms (phenomenal existence)

Intrinsic to phenomenal existence is the primordial nature that is described as suchness, inherent nature, Dharma nature, prajna wisdom, nirvana, and wholesomeness without outflows. Huineng, the Sixth Patriarch of Chinese Chan Buddhism, famously exclaimed, "Who could have thought intrinsic nature is inherently so pure and clear! Who could have thought intrinsic nature is inherently complete!" This is similar to the lights of the Pure Land of all Buddhas shining together as one without any obstruction, or the light of the Pure Land of the Medicine Buddha that is intensely bright, pure and flawless.

To have attained the complete and perfect state of the Dharma realm is to say that the Dharma body of the Buddha is devoid of all notions of relativity or duality. It is a state that transcends time and space, birth and death, you and me, and love and hatred. It the elimination of the mundane desires of the "Great Perfect Mirror-like Wisdom" as expounded in the doctrine of "Consciousness Only," the non-birth and non-death of the Tathagatagarbha as explained in the *Treatise on the Awakening of Faith in Mahayana*,[99] the Dharma rain of one taste[100] that benefits all allegorized in the *Lotus Sutra*, and the severing of all outflows without any attachment depicted by the Chan School. Such existence is completely free from impurities, and is neither born nor extinguished. It is beneficial to all, and not bound by any attachments. This is the state of complete and perfect attainment of the bodhisattva path.

The Dharma realm may be vast, yet it is all within the mind, is capable of embracing space and worlds as numerous as the sands of the Ganges, penetrating hell or shuttling through the heavens. However, such a mind must be nourished by the wisdom and merit accumulated through a very long period of cultivation on the bodhisattva path.

---

[99] The *Great Treatise on the Awakening of Faith in Mahayana* was believed to have been written by Asvaghosa Bodhisattva and translated by Zhendi of the Southern Dynasty. It teaches the dependent origination of the Tathagatagarbha and states that the minds of sentient beings neither arises nor ceases, is beyond expression in language, and is ultimately equal and unchanging.

[100] Meaning all things and doctrines are equal without differentiation. It often points to the Buddha's teachings.

Glossary

Amitabha Buddha: Used in English to represent two Sanskrit terms: "Amitaba" ("Infinite Light") and "Amitayus" ("Infinite Life"). Amitabha is the Buddha of compassion and wisdom and is one of the most popular Buddhas in Mahayana Buddhism. He presides over the Western Pure Land of Ultimate Bliss.

Ananda: One of the ten great disciples of the Buddha. He is noted as foremost in hearing and learning.

arhat: Literally, a "Worthy one." The noble person who has eliminated all afflictions and passions and has attained the fourth level of the supramundane path. An arhat will no longer be subject to rebirth.

asamkheyakalpa: A period of time equal to an incalculably large number of kalpas.

asuras: Demigods. One of the six kinds of beings that reside in the six realms of existence.

bhiksu: The male members of the sangha, who have renounced household life and received full ordination.

bhiksuni: The female members of the sangha, who have renounced household life and received full ordination.

bodhi: It means enlightenment. In the state of enlightenment, one is awakened to the true nature of self; one is enlightened to one's own Buddha nature. Such a person has already eliminated all afflictions and delusions, and achieved prajna wisdom.

bodhicitta: Literally, "bodhi mind." The mind that seeks enlightenment.

Brahman: In ancient India, the highest of four castes.

Buddha: Literally, "Enlightened one." When "the Buddha" is used, it usually refers to the historical Buddha, Sakyamuni Buddha.

Buddhahood: The state and condition of being a Buddha. Buddhahood is the ultimate goal of all beings.

causes and conditions: Referring to the primary cause (causes) and the secondary causes (conditions). The seed out of which a plant or a flower grows is a good illustration of a primary cause; the elements of soil, humidity, sunlight, and so forth, could be considered secondary causes.

Chan School: One school of Chinese Buddhism. Founded by Bodhidharma, it emphasizes the cultivation of intrinsic wisdom, and teaches that enlightenment is clarifying the mind and seeing one's own true nature. Another tenant of the Chan School is that the Dharma is wordlessly transmitted from mind to mind.

cycle of birth and death: *Skt. "samsara"* or *"jatimarana."* When sentient beings die, they are reborn into one of the six realms of existence (heaven, the human realm, the asura realm, the animal realm, the realm of hungry ghost and hell). The cycle is continuous and endless due to the karmic result of one's deeds.

dependent origination: The central principle of Buddhism that phenomena do not come into existence independently but only as a result of causes and conditions; therefore, no phenomena possess an independent self-nature. This concept is also referred to as interdependence.

devas: Celestial beings. One of the six kinds of beings that reside in the six realms of existence.

Dharma: The capitalized form refers to the ultimate truth and the teachings of the Buddha. When it appears in lowercase, it refers to anything that can be thought of, experienced, or named; "phenomena."

Dharma body: *Skt. "Dharmakaya;"* refers to the true nature of a Buddha, and also to the absolute Dharma that the Buddha attained. It is one of three bodies possessed by a Buddha.

Dharma nature: The true nature of all phenomena. Equivalent in meaning to "suchness" and "emptiness."

dharma realm: *Skt. "dharma-dhatu."* It indicates the notion of true nature that encompasses all phenomena. As a space or realm of dharmas, it is the uncaused and immutable totality in which all phenomena arise, abide and cease to be.

Dharma Wheel: The wheel of the Dharma, it symbolizes the teaching of the Buddha which can crush all delusion and affliction like a wheel rolling on. The wheel's roundness is also meant to symbolize perfection.

Dr. Sun Yat Sen: The father of the Republic of China.

emptiness: *Skt.* "*sunya*;" a concept in Buddhism that states that everything existing in the world arises due to dependent origination and has no permanent self or substance. It can be categorized into two groups: 1) emptiness of people (living beings), which means that human beings or other living beings have no unchanging, substantial self; and 2) emptiness of dharmas, which means that the existence of all phenomena are due to causes and conditions.

enlightenment: The state of awakening to the Truth—freedom from all affliction and suffering.

Five aggregates: Indicates form, feeling, perception, mental formation and consciousness.

Five great violations: Patricide, matricide, killing an arhat, shedding the blood of a Buddha and destroying the harmony of the sangha.

Four Means of Embracing: *Skt.* "*catvari-samgraha-vastuni.*" The four methods that bodhisattvas use to guide sentient beings to the path of liberation: giving, kind words, altruism and beneficence, and sympathy and empathy.

Four Noble Truths: A fundamental and essential teaching of Buddhism that describes the presence of suffering, the cause of suffering, the path leading to the cessation of suffering, and the cessation of suffering.

Gandharan Art: Gandhara is the name of an ancient kingdom, located in northern Pakistan, Jammu and Kashmir and eastern Afghanistan. Gandharan art is a style of Buddhist art, which developed out of a merging of Greek, Syrian, Persian, Chinese and Indian artistic influences.

gatha: Verses.

Great Compassion Dharani: *Skt.* "*Mahakarunikacitta-dharani.*" The dharani of the merits and virtues of Avalokitesvara. According to the sutras, sincerely reciting this dharani 108 times can eliminate unwholesome karmas and purify the body and mind.

Hinayana Buddhism: Also known as the "Small Vehicle" or "Lesser Vehicle." Literally, it means the vehicle that can only carry a few people. This term is used to refer to one who only focuses on self-cultivation.

Huayan School: School of Buddhism in China which focuses on the *Avatamsaka Sutra*.

impermanence: One of the most basic truths taught by the Buddha. It is the concept that all conditioned dharmas, or phenomena, will arise, abide, change and disappear due to causes and conditions.

kalpa: The measuring unit of time in ancient India; a kalpa is an immense and inconceivable length of time.

karma: This means "work, action or deeds." All deeds, whether good or bad, produce effects. The effects may be experienced instantly, or they may not come into fruition for many years or even many lifetimes.

King Asoka: He reigned as the King of the Maurya Kingdom in India from 272–236 BCE. He was the foremost royal patron of Buddhism in India and the first monarch to rule over a united India.

Mahayana Buddhism: Mahayana literally means "Great Vehicle," one of the main traditions of Buddhism. Mahayana Buddhism stresses that helping other sentient beings to achieve enlightenment is as important as self-liberation.

Mahakasyapa: One of the ten great disciples of the Buddha. He is known as the foremost in the practice of asceticism. He is considered the First Chan Patriarch.

Maitreya's Pure Land: The inner palace at Tusita Heaven, where Maitreya Bodhisattva presides and expounds the Dharma to celestial beings.

Mara: The Destroyer, the Evil One.

merit: The blessings of wealth, health, intelligence, etc., which are accrued by benefiting others and by practicing what is good.

nirvana: The absolute extinction of individual existence, or of all afflictions and desires; it is the state of liberation, beyond birth and death. It is also the final goal in Buddhism.

non-self: *Skt.* "*anatman*" or "*niratman.*" The basic Buddhist concept that all phenomena and beings in the world have no real, permanent or substantial self.

parinirvana: A synonym for nirvana. It is the state of having completed all merits and perfections and eliminated all unwholesomeness. Usually, it is used to refer the passing away of a Buddha.

prajna wisdom: Prajna wisdom is the highest form of wisdom. It is the wisdom of insight into the true nature of all phenomena.

pratyekabuddha: Solitary awakened one; one who attains enlightenment on his own, without having heard the teachings of a Buddha.

precepts: Vows of morality taken by Buddhists as the foundation of Buddhist practice. There are different sets of precepts for monastics and lay practitioners.

Pure Land: Another term for a Buddha realm, which is established by the vows and cultivation of one who has achieved enlightenment.

Saha world: The present world where we reside, which is full of suffering that must be endured. The beings in this world endure suffering and afflictions due to their greed, anger, hatred and ignorance.

Sakyamuni Buddha: The historical founder of Buddhism. He was born the prince of Kapilavastu, son of King Suddhodana. At the age of twenty-nine, he left the royal palace and his family to search for the meaning of existence. At the age of thirty-five, he attained enlightenment under the bodhi tree. He then spent the next forty-five years expounding his teachings, which include the Four Noble Truths, the Noble Eightfold Path, the Law of Cause and Effect, and dependent origination. At the age of eighty, he entered the state of *parinirvana*.

samadhi: A state in which the mind is concentrated with one-pointed focus and all mental activities are calm. In samadhi, one's mind is free from all distractions and enters a state of inner serenity.

sangha: Indicating the Buddhist community; in a broad sense it includes both monastics and laypeople. However, most often it refers to the monastics.

Sariputra: One of the Buddha's ten great disciples, he is known as the foremost in wisdom.

Sanskrit: Ancient Indian language.

sentient beings: *Skt. "sattvas."* All beings with consciousness, including celestial beings, asuras, humans, animals, hungry ghosts, and hellish beings. From a Mahayana perspective, all sentient beings inherently have Buddha nature and therefore possess the capacity to attain enlightenment.

Six Perfections: Six practices of a bodhisattva: giving, upholding precepts, patience, diligence, meditation, and prajna wisdom.

six realms of existence: Heaven, the human realm, the *asura* realm, the animal realm, the realm of hungry ghosts, and hell.

sravaka: One who has attained enlightenment after listening to the Buddha's teachings.

stupa: A dome shaped monument used to house Buddhist relics or to commemorate significant events in Buddhism.

suchness: A term for the true nature of all things; the pure, original essence of all phenomena, which is called *tathata* or *bhuta-tathata*. It is a central notion of Mahayana Buddhism.

sutra: The scriptures taught by the Buddha.

Tathagata: One of the ten epithets of the Buddha, literally translated as "Thus-Come One," meaning the one who has attained full realization of suchness.

Ten Powers of Tathagata: Having complete knowledge of: 1) what is right or wrong in every condition; 2) what is the karma of every being, past, present, and future; 3) all stages of dhyana liberation, and samadhi; 4) the faculties and capacities of all beings; 5) the dispositions of all beings; 6) the actual condition of every individual; 7) the direction and consequence of all laws; 8) all causes of mortality and of good and evil in their reality; 9) the death and rebirth of all beings; 10) the destruction of all illusions of every kind.

Thirty-seven practices to enlightenment: These include four applications of mindfulness, four right efforts, four bases of spiritual power, five faculties, five powers, seven limbs of enlightenment and the Eightfold Noble Truth.

Thirty-two Marks of Excellence: Remarkable physical characteristics possessed by a Buddha; the symbols of qualities attained at the highest level of cultivation.

Three Dharma Seals: Three truths about reality: all conditioned dharmas are impermanent, all dharmas are without self, and nirvana is perfect tranquility.

three time periods: The past, the present and the future.

Three Vehicles: The three divisions of the Buddha's teachings: 1) the *sravakayana*, in which one realizes and practices the Four Noble Truths and attains arhatship; 2) the *pratyekabuddhayana*, in which one realizes and practices the Twelve Links of Causation and becomes a pratyekabuddha; 3) the *bodhisattvayana*, in which one attains ultimate Buddhahood after countless kalpas of practice.

Tripitaka: The Buddhist Canon. It is divided into three categories: the sutras (teachings of the Buddha), the vinaya (precepts and rules), and the abhidharma (commentaries on the Buddha's teachings).

Triple Gem: The Buddha, the Dharma, and the Sangha.

upasaka: A lay male Buddhist follower.

upasika: A female lay Buddhist follower.

Vairocana Buddha: His name literally means "He who is like the sun," symbolizing the greatness of the Buddha's wisdom. He is regarded as the embodiment of Dharma.

vajra: A diamond-like substance that is indestructible and powerful.

vihara: The residence of a religious practitioner; a temple.

vinaya: The monastic discipline maintained by the Buddhist community. This term can also refer to the *vinaya-pitaka*, the collected literature that enumerates and discusses these rules.

Western Pure Land of Ultimate Bliss: The realm where Amitabha Buddha presides, created from Amitahba Buddha's forty-eight great vows. Sentient beings can vow to be reborn here, where they can practice without obstructions until they attain enlightenment.

Xuanzang: A great master of the Tang Dynasty, he is one of four great translators in Buddhist history. He studied in India for seventeen years and was responsible for bringing many collections of works, images, pictures, as well as one hundred and fifty relics, to China from India. One of his most famous works is the *Buddhist Records of the Western Regions.*

About the Author

Founder of the Fo Guang Shan (Buddha's Light Mountain) Buddhist Order and the Buddha's Light International Association, Venerable Master Hsing Yun has dedicated his life to teaching Humanistic Buddhism, which seeks to realize spiritual cultivation in everyday living.

Master Hsing Yun is the 48th Patriarch of the Linji Chan School. Born in Jiangsu Province, China in 1927, he was tonsured under Venerable Master Zhikai at the age of twelve and became a novice monk at Qixia Vinaya College. He was fully ordained in 1941 following years of strict monastic training. When he left Jiaoshan Buddhist College at the age of twenty, he had studied for almost ten years in a monastery.

Due to the civil war in China, Master Hsing Yun moved to Taiwan in 1949 where he undertook the revitalization of Chinese Mahayana Buddhism. He began fulfilling his vow to promote the Dharma by starting chanting groups, student and youth groups, and other civic-minded organizations with Leiyin Temple in Ilan as his base. Since the founding of Fo Guang Shan monastery in Kaohsiung in 1967, more than two hundred temples have been established worldwide. Hsi Lai Temple, the symbolic torch of the

Dharma spreading to the West, was built in 1988 near Los Angeles.

Master Hsing Yun has been guiding Buddhism on a course of modernization by integrating Buddhist values into education, cultural activities, charity, and religious practices. To achieve these ends, he travels all over the world, giving lectures and actively engaging in religious dialogue. The Fo Guang Shan organization also oversees sixteen Buddhist colleges and four universities, one of which is the University of the West in Rosemead, California.

Other Works by Venerable Master Hsing Yun:

Being Good
Infinite Compassion, Endless Wisdom
Footprints in the Ganges
Traveling to the other Shore
The Core Teachings
Where is Your Buddha Nature?
Humanistic Buddhism: A Blueprint for Life
Chan Heart, Chan Art
Humble Table, Wise Fare

About the Publisher

As long as Venerable Master Hsing Yun has been a Buddhist monk, he has had a strong belief that books and other documentation of the Buddha's teachings unite us emotionally, help us practice Buddhism at a higher level, and continuously challenge our views on how we define our lives

In 1996, the Fo Guang Shan International Translation Center was established with this goal in mind. This marked the beginning of a string of publications translated into various languages from the Master's original writings in Chinese. Presently, several trans-lation centers have been set up worldwide. Centers that coordinate translation or publication projects are located in Los Angeles and San Diego, USA; Sydney, Australia; Berlin, Germany; Argentina; South Africa; and Japan.

In 2001, Buddha's Light Publishing was established to publish Buddhist books translated by the Fo Guang Shan International Translation Center as well as other valuable Buddhist works. Buddha's Light Publishing is committed to building bridges between East and West, Buddhist communities, and cultures. All proceeds from our book sales support Buddhist propagation efforts.